WELL...
I GUESS
I'M NOT
JESUS

A TRUE STORY

ADAM HELBLING

TO MY MOM

THE MOST BEAUTIFUL PERSON INSIDE AND OUT.

FOR BEING THERE FOR ME EVERY STEP OF THE WAY.

THE STRONGEST WOMAN I KNOW.

YOU WERE MY STRENGTH WHEN I WAS WEAK.

A MOTHER COULD NOT LOVE A SON ANYMORE THAN YOU CAN.

I WOULD NOT BE WHERE I AM AT WITHOUT YOU.

I LOVE YOU MORE THAN ANYTHING.

CONTENTS

ACKNOWLEDGMENTS

Thank you for the support of my friends and family who helped me to get through this crazy journey. A very special thank you to my parents, Patsy and Bob Helbling, who have been there for me every step of the way. I would like to thank The Ohio State University for providing me with so many tremendous opportunities over the years. A very special thank you to Creative Living for helping me to live independently and for helping me pursue my dreams in Columbus. To Jon Giganti and Patty Shook for all of their help with this project. Thank you to Gretchen Hirsch for the tremendous job she did editing this book and making it a more cohesive narrative. To Chris Casella for the photograph on the cover and to Kate Johnson for the cover design. To Rob Musil of Artfall Studio for the inside illustration.

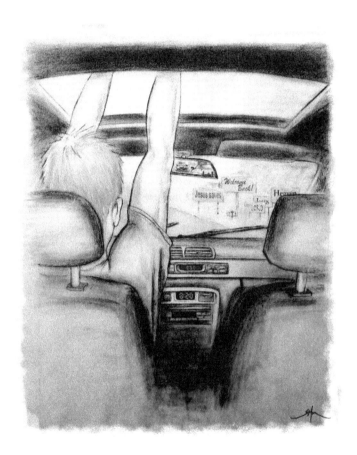

INTRODUCTION

I've always thought ahead. I set a goal, achieved it, and moved on to the next. I laid out my life and worked toward my dreams, one step at a time. I could see myself five, ten, even fifteen years down the road, and I engaged in a relentless pursuit of what I wanted to accomplish next.

But life turns on a dime. If I were playing poker, I'd say that until I was 24 years old, I held a royal flush—in spades. But in one split second, I was left with a pair of twos. What I've discovered, however, is that if you play it right, a pair of twos can win.

PREFACE

When I was three years old, I started waterskiing on the front of my dad's skis. By age six I was skiing on one ski. Every spring break my family would take a vacation down to Winter Haven, Florida, to start the season off early. Being from Ohio, I did not have the luxury of skiing year-round. But once it got the slightest bit warm, I was on the water. I spent nearly every weekend of every summer camping and skiing on the Clarion River in Pennsylvania. I had a girlfriend from second to sixth grade, and what kept us together was waterskiing.

On the Clarion I was king of the slalom course. Boats would park close to the course just to watch me ski, and that was the greatest feeling in the world. I always dreamed of skiing for Sea World, which was only 30 minutes from my house. Once I got old enough to realize my dream, the park shut down and the water ski shows were dead and gone.

I found the next best thing, though. When I was 16, I joined a water-ski show team in Akron, Ohio. We put on an hour-long show for the public every Wednesday in the summer. The show consisted of all types of skiing stunts, from jumping to barefooting to four-tier pyramids. In my second year with the team, in 2004, we won the Division II Show Ski National Championship.

I spent three years with the team before going on to focus solely on my real passion: slalom skiing. In 2007, I spent the entire summer in Maine teaching kids how to waterski. Back home in Ohio, I found an open invitation to several private waterski lakes, which gave me a great deal of time to practice the sport. In the summer of 2008, I won the Ohio Water Ski Association Men's I State Slalom Championship. My father had won that championship nearly 30 years before, and it was always something I wanted to achieve, too.

I graduated from high school in 2005 and went on to attend The Ohio State University on a full scholarship. I worked hard in high school and my high GPA—more than a 4.0—and my involvement in extracurricular activities led to my receiving a scholarship from the Ohio State's Office of Minority Affairs. I was awarded the scholarship because I was a first-generation college student, not because I'm a minority. Let's be honest: waterskiing is the whitest sport in the world.

I joined the OSU waterski team my first week of school, and my leadership abilities grew with my membership on the team. Within three weeks of joining, I ran for captain of the team, even though I knew I didn't have a shot in hell. I saw it as an opportunity for me to introduce myself to the team and show that I wanted to get involved.

I lost, which was no surprise to me, but afterwards the officers told me they needed people like me. They said to stick around and that my time would come. That was true; later that year an opening came up for treasurer, and I ran and won. The next year I ran for captain of the team, and this time around I was victorious. I was even elected to a second term during my junior year.

The University gave us less than $1,000 a year for the organization, which was nothing for such an expensive sport. The first step, then, was to raise money for a new boat. Eventually we were successful in purchasing a 2002 Mastercraft ProStar 209 that cost $32,000. This purchase led to great development of our team.

By my final ski season at Ohio State, I recruited for our men's team at summer tournaments. Our men's team was stacked, but our women's team still needed some work. I spent the entire spring, summer, and fall training our women's team to get ready for competition. That fall we qualified for nationals for the first time in 23 years and traveled to Austin, Texas, where we won the USA Waterski Division II Collegiate National Championship.

The water ski team wasn't the only thing I did at Ohio State. I'm the type of person who says yes to anything; when I was asked to get involved with an organization, I got on board immediately. I was quickly building an extensive résumé at Ohio State, making a name for myself, and meeting hundreds of new people. I became a member of Sphinx, the senior class honorary; Texnikoi Engineering Honorary; the Honors Program; the Mount Leadership Society (OSU Scholars Program); Phi Kappa Psi; and the Morrill Scholars Program.

How, with all this success, did I end up in a mental hospital, telling everyone I was Jesus Christ—and believing it? Drugs had a part in it, of course, and so did that fact that I was diagnosed with bipolar disorder. The combination of those two factors led me to an even darker place—an accident that left me paralyzed, with partial use of only one arm.

I've written this book in hopes of reaching the lost and the scared, the depressed and the anxious. I want to help people realize just how much they have and encourage them to live life, whatever its shape and limits, to the fullest. My goal is to make people smile, laugh at themselves, and forget about their flaws. To prod them into trying something new and not to be scared that others may be watching them fail. Success requires some failures along the way.

Certainly I've succeeded, and I've also screwed up along the way. I've made my family proud—and frightened them to death. I've hit rock bottom twice. I climbed my way back to the top once and I am working on doing that again.

This is my story, and I hope it will bring light and inspiration.

SECTION I

-1-
WAKING UP

When I opened my eyes, I knew I was Jesus Christ, but I had no idea where I was. I was pretty sure it was a hospital, but since there were no crazy wires or tubes attached to me, I thought that was good news. The guy in the next bed looked fine, too. He was sleeping. I yelled at him to wake up, and he finally rolled over to face me.

It was my best friend, Kyle, or so I thought. I stared at him, laughing hysterically, and he stared back at me, confused as hell. I couldn't believe my friend was in the hospital, too, right next to me. True, he didn't look *exactly* like my friend, but I thought that was because he'd been dressed up Hollywood-style. He was much chubbier than usual, which I thought the make-up artists had pulled off with latex and some kind of body padding. I got up and walked over to his bed and started pulling at his face. He hollered at me to stop tugging his cheeks. He was royally pissed, but I thought it was all an act.

I had yet to recognize that I was in a psych ward, so I decided to walk around the hospital a little bit. After all, I was Jesus. I was untouchable and knew I could do whatever the hell I wanted.

Not only was I Jesus, but I also knew I was on some kind of reality TV show the rest of the world was watching. The signs of it were everywhere—and I kept looking for more. My mind was whirling out of control, and this time I couldn't get it back.

HOW I GOT TO WHERE I WAS

The day I entered the psych ward was October 24, 2008, and it had been a long time coming. I was not nearly as crazy during my freshman year in college as I was in the years to come. I would drink only on the weekends, but when I drank I did it to get hammered. The house parties at Ohio State were always huge, sometimes more than 100-keggers. Freshmen never paid for anything, and the beer was always free. Of course, it was either Natural Light or Keystone, but it always did the trick.

Many a night I came back to my dorm just to lock myself in the bathroom and stick my head in the toilet. The shower was right next to the toilet, and on occasion I would clog the drain with towels and lie down in the shower with my head in the toilet. I could fill the shower up to about six inches, so I would lie in the warm pube-infested water while throwing up until I passed out. Eventually one of my roommates would find me lying naked in the nasty water and send me to bed.

For a while, I was fascinated with fireworks. One night, I wanted to show a friend how a certain firecracker could blow up under water. I lit it and tossed it into the toilet. It exploded—and the toilet came off the wall and shattered into a thousand pieces. The next day I put in a maintenance request to have the toilet replaced. When the maintenance man asked me what happened, I told him I sat on it and it broke off the wall.

He apologized and said that happened more often than people thought.

Later that week, blitzed again, I decided to shoot off some Roman candles. I stuck one on a grate outside my dorm and lit it. As soon as it went off, it fell into a pile of dried leaves near the basement window. The leaves went up in flames. I decided that pissing on the fire was the best option to put it out. But soon I ran out of piss, and my friends and I ran inside to find water. We put the fire out, thank God, because if we hadn't, that probably would have been my last day at Ohio State.

Although I stayed away from pot most of my freshman year, I did smoke from time to time. I was still terrified of it because a couple years before I had smoked something I think was laced. My heart was beating out of my chest and I thought I was going to have a heart attack. But in the years to come, marijuana would become a huge part of my life.

-2-
HELL WEEK SENDS ME THERE

When I was accepted at Ohio State, I received an application for the Freshman Excellence Scholarship, an award offered by Phi Kappa Psi fraternity. A few months later, I received a letter in the mail saying that I was one of 20 finalists who would be interviewed to receive one of the four scholarships.

An interview was scheduled at the Phi Kappa Psi fraternity house. I later found out that I was chosen to receive one of the four $500 scholarships, which, since my school was already paid for, I used to buy a brand-new iPod.

They invited me to a ceremony where they gave out the scholarships. Then they showed us around the fraternity and pushed hard to recruit us to become pledges. I had no interest in joining a fraternity. I already had several outlets to make friends, so I wasn't ready to pay for them. But I did take them up on the offer to come to their parties.

The parties were after hours, and the house would fill up with hundreds of people. The guy-to-girl ratio was ridiculous—ten girls for every guy. The parties were a lot of fun and it was a great way to meet girls, except that sorority girls were interested only in meeting guys who were active members of a fraternity.

I resisted joining during fall quarter and winter

quarter, but when they pushed me to join spring quarter, I finally gave in. I became a pledge in spring 2006 and convinced my best friend, Kyle, to join with me. However, after pledging, I discovered I was working toward something I later found to a complete waste of my time. I spent every week washing dishes and catering to the brothers. I was required clean the house, which was a giant, disgusting old governor's mansion. People would shave their pubes in the sink and throw up in the showers. Pledges had to unclog toilets and scrub every inch of the bathrooms.

Several times throughout the quarter, actives crammed the 20+ pledges into a room and blindfolded us. For two to three hours, we had to sit in the dark and listen to "The End" by The Doors. This song haunts me to this day.

The final part of pledging, held during summer quarter so the hazing would be less obvious, was Hell Week, or what they called Inspiration I-Week. To start off I-Week, we were required to buy our big brother a weapon and a porno. I went to the local Army surplus store, found a set of ninja stars, and then went on a search for the perfect porno. At a pawn shop with Kyle, I came across the nastiest video I'd ever seen, and I'm happy to say I never watched it with my big brother.

Next we had to go to the store with our pledge brothers and buy a long list of items we would need for that week, including things such as adult diapers and laxatives: things that would make us imagine what was to come. When we returned to the house, we gave up our cell phones and wallets. We were to have no connection to the outside world for the coming week.

During the day we spent our time cleaning the

house and doing random chores. Nighttime was a rude awakening.

Physically I was more ready than anybody for Hell Week. I was in the best shape of my life. But mentally I wasn't ready, as I only started studying the information we were supposed to know about each active brother two days before the dreaded week started—and that information was extensive.

On that first night, they lined us up alphabetically in the basement of the fraternity. We had to keep our toes on a line and look up at the ceiling for the entire night. Horrible scream-o music was blasting through my giant Peavey amp, which they used without my permission.

The brothers flooded into the basement, and one by one they would come up to us and scream questions until someone got one wrong, and that pledge would have to do an absurd number of push-ups or wall squats—all designed to break us down physically until we broke down mentally.

As the week went on, we were tested and tested again under strobe lights—and we couldn't leave until we answered the questions correctly. Each night they got harder. After eight hours of sheer hell, we were allowed to go to sleep until about 5 A.M. Bed, though, was the hard tile floor. My mind raced. I couldn't sleep, but it didn't matter, because two hours later the brothers were back, blasting that god-awful music again. It was time for the onions. We were forced to eat giant onions that make you sick unless they're cooked. Guys were puking everywhere. One passed out.

There was more. After the onions and the vomiting, it was time to work out. And then a shower, during which we were covered in shampoo and not given enough time to rinse it off. It itched all day.

I went all the way through Hell Week, day after day. When it was over, all I wanted to do was sleep, but the brothers insisted we party because the week was finished. I went over to one of the fraternity brother's houses where they were pouring shot after shot of Jack Daniels. It was that night that I found out I'm allergic to Jack Daniels. I spent the entire next day on their couch or wandering back and forth to the bathroom. I threw up all day long, and Jack Daniels made me shit black.

Hell Week didn't bond me to anyone. It made me hate the fraternity. All I wanted to do was get out. Most of my pledge class was living elsewhere, and now I was surrounded by the people who just spent an entire week hazing the shit out of me. This would never feel like home to me. I was miserable, and my mind was shot. I fell into a deep depression, which lasted for the entire 10-week autumn quarter.

During all of autumn quarter of my sophomore year, I was more depressed than I had ever been in my life. I called my mom at least five times a day. I went to the doctor and got on antidepressants, but even those didn't do anything for me. I needed to get out of the fraternity. I could not live there any longer.

-3-
A NEW HOME. A NEW PERSON.

I spent the end of autumn quarter looking for a new place to live. At Ohio State, the students usually find housing a year ahead of time, so I knew my options would be limited. I'd heard about some brand-new townhouses I wanted to check out, but I knew I probably could not afford one. Nonetheless, I went in during an open house and sat down and talked to the landlord. These were probably the nicest places to live on campus. The problem was that they were three- and four-bedroom townhouses and the landlord was asking between $2,100 and $2,400 per month. In spite of that, I took a tour of the place and loved it.

At the end of the tour, I talked to the landlord and told her I really was looking for a one-bedroom, but I wanted to move out immediately. She said she might be able to help me. The company had just finished building the townhouses in December, and since most students were already in leases, the leasing company was trying to get whatever they could for them. I explained to her that I could afford to pay only about $500 a month for the place.

I couldn't believe she was willing to accept my offer and that I could move in at the beginning of the new year. For $500 a month I was going to have three bedrooms, two bathrooms, and a three-car garage. The master bedroom even had a huge balcony. I could see all the way to downtown Columbus from my apartment. I couldn't wait to live there.

I told my fraternity I wouldn't be living there for the rest of the school year, and with that settled, I began the long climb out of my deep depression. I spent winter break calling family and friends to see if they had any furniture they didn't want, and I also found some on Craigslist. I was ready for the move.

Of course, I made the master bedroom my room. The other upstairs bedroom became a guest bedroom, and the downstairs bedroom was my office. With this new living arrangement, I had gone from sharing an old, nasty room in a frat house with two other guys to having more space than I ever could have dreamed of.

No one ever wanted to visit me in the fraternity. I always had to go out of my way to see my friends. But now my place was very popular. I went from being absolutely miserable and depressed to the happiest kid on campus. From being way down, I start to go way up. I had spent so much time being miserable that now all I wanted to do was enjoy my life. I did, but I lost control of it, too.

Many of my friends were still living in the dorms for their sophomore year, so they needed a place to party. My apartment became the place where they went to get away from the rules and restrictions of dorm life. It was where we started to smoke weed on a regular basis—and though I loved weed, it was the beginning of a lot of problems.

I had way too much fun for the six months I lived in the apartment. Once it got warmer, I took the boat out before class to ski. Because I never wanted to get off the boat, I would stay out and skip all my classes. When exams came around, I was always so far behind I had to cram for everything.

I started to rely on Adderall to study for my classes. As an engineering major, I had a great deal to learn for each test. Adderall was like steroids for studying. I could study for 12 hours straight and enjoy every minute of it. I felt like a mad scientist, completing problem after problem. I ended up doing surprisingly well on my exams, but after the exams I'd find that I couldn't retain any of the information. It wasn't the best way to get through school.

BPT

Most of the townhouses around me were empty, and those that were occupied were pretty quiet. I was ready to change that pattern and start having parties. As I changed that pattern, I took a few steps closer to the abyss. I didn't want to pay for the parties I planned, so my friends and I came up with an ingenious strategy.

Beer pong was very popular at the time, and we decided we were going to throw beer pong tournaments. The first tournament was for 16 teams and each person paid $5 to play. We used the money to buy the beer, and we gave a small cash prize to the winning team. We bought a bunch of sawhorses and pieces of plywood to make five tables. We bought poster board to draw the brackets, and we set up everything in the garage. I used my giant Peavey amp to blast music. I set up a room for a hookah I'd bought. However, the hookah room was a bad idea; the hookah spilled multiple times and the coals burned giant holes in my carpet. Unfortunately, that was just the beginning of the end of my luxury home.

After the first tournament, people demanded that I throw more of them, so on I went to BPT 2.0. I advertised the tournament on Facebook asking for 32 teams, but more than 40 signed up. Week after week, people demanded that I have another tournament. After the second one, I decided to host a 64-team tournament. With the help of Facebook again, the tournament filled up; but the hardest part was collecting $5 from each of the 128 people who would be playing. I finally had more than $600 to spend on this party, so I spent $500 on beer, which left $100 for the winning team. Because I was only 20 years old, I couldn't buy the beer, so I had a friend with a fake ID come with me to a drive-through, where we loaded up his pickup truck with $500 worth of Keystone.

The 64-team tournaments were outrageous. The first floor of my apartment was always packed. People were baking out in my closet upstairs. The guest bedroom turned into a sex room, probably because I had bowls of condoms laid out. I used to work at a place that sold 50 condoms for $5, so I stocked up and gave them away. The hookah room was a huge hit. Eventually I built a wooden frame around the hookah so it wouldn't spill, but by that time it didn't matter. The carpet was already trashed and would have to be replaced. In the kitchen, I had a bar set up, and behind the bar gorgeous sorority girls passed out the beer. They had a list of everyone in the tournament, and anyone not on the list had to tip the girls. Downstairs in the garage, the music pounded as the tournament went on.

I would get blind at these parties. Hammered. Stoned. Yet I was still able to manage organizing a 64-

team tournament. The biggest problem I had was trying not to spend the prize money that was supposed to go to the winning team. I lived right across from a gas station and when I ran out of beer, I'd have someone go there to buy more. We always ran out of hookah tobacco, too, so I'd have to find somebody sober enough to drive my car to the hookah bar for another supply. Party after party resulted in the destruction of my house.

Not only that, but people also stole the most random things from me. Someone stole an area rug out from under a giant coffee table, and someone else stole my barstools. For one party, I hid everything anyone would want to steal, but someone still managed to rip off my disco ball. I saw one kid walking out of my apartment with a giant cardboard Halo 2 poster. He wasn't at all discreet about it, so I grabbed the poster from him and threw him down my front steps.

I was getting so fed up with people stealing things. On the morning after one of the parties, I realized that my giant, pink, five-foot-tall gumball machine was missing. How could somebody possibly walk out of a party with something that large? Soon enough I found out how. I was working out at the rec center when I got a call from my landlord saying that there were people in my apartment. She wondered if they should be there. I said no and told her to call the cops. It turned out to be just a group of my friends who had broken into my place to return the gumball machine. When the landlord called me back, I told her to cancel the cops.

When I got home, my friends explained to me how they had stolen it in the first place. The machine was in the office/hookah room, which had a back balcony. They parked their pickup truck below the balcony and then lowered the gumball machine into the truck and drove away. I wasn't mad at all because I thought it was a great prank.

I threw seven beer pong tournaments before I moved out in June. I also had several other parties—and the apartment was a disaster. The walls had black marks all over them from people rubbing against them. I also did a few things myself to screw up the place. At one of the parties I got so drunk and high that at the end of the night I pulled a giant bush out of the ground, dragged it inside, and threw it across my living room into the kitchen. It left a ton of dirt behind all of the appliances.

Some of the worst damage happened, though, when I threw a party for the Phi Psi pledge class. They approached me about having a party with the Pi Beta Phi sorority pledge class. The Pi Phis were the best-looking sorority on campus, so of course I was up for it. It was a Boone's Farm party and they bought enough of that wine to fill my entire fridge. I guess some guys get violent when they drink that girly wine. Someone punched giant holes in the wall in my garage, the wall coming up the basement steps, and another—the largest—in my living room wall. I was so pissed—and no one would man up and confess. Some people promised to fix it, but that day never came.

The next party also involved my fraternity, but I think the damage was my fault. Phi Psi has an event every spring called the Phi Psi 500. They flooded the front yard of the fraternity and made it a giant mud pit. The event started at noon, but different sororities "pregamed" at some of the actives' houses. My place was chosen as a pregame spot. So at 8 A.M., about 20 sorority girls came knocking on my door.

My friend Jason had crashed on my couch the night before because we'd been up until 5 A.M. I forgot to tell Jason that the girls were going to show up at eight that morning. When he answered the door, he was in shock, but he managed to rise to the occasion, and the party started over. It didn't take long for me to get drunk because I was still drunk from the night before. In a few minutes, I was taking bong hits and shots; I was gone within the first hour.

At that point, I thought it would be a good idea to bring out the fireworks. I lit a bottle rocket and shot it through the party. Everyone was so drunk they barely noticed, except for one girl, who blasted out of the hookah room with her purse on fire from the bottle rocket that had flown into it and left a gaping hole.

She was furious because she had just bought the purse. I told her that since I destroyed one of her things she could destroy something of mine. I pointed to the hole in the living room wall and told her to go to town. Soon enough there was a bunch of girls beating the hell out of my wall, and Jason was there to help, too. The hole went from being about a square foot to about four feet tall by three feet wide. I was so messed up I didn't even care. That seemed to be the norm for me in those days, which is why I think so many people loved coming over. They knew they could do anything they wanted.

FACING EVICTION

Clearly the house was in no shape for inspection, but since I was nearing the end of my lease, I had to get ready for one—on very short notice. I tried to cover up the giant hole in my living room with a poster, but, of course, it didn't work.

The inspection came when I was away for the weekend, and when I got home, my landlord told me the inspector wanted to evict me right then, less than two weeks before I was scheduled to move out. The landlord talked the inspector into letting me stay and fix the place up.

I got down to work right away, beginning at Lowe's, where I bought boxes of Mr. Clean Magic Erasers to get the black marks off the walls. The walls were so bad in the garage that I decided to paint them. I also rented a carpet-cleaning machine to clean the steps going down to the garage, the steps going upstairs, and the entire upstairs. I left the first floor alone because I knew all that carpet would have to be replaced. I bought drywall and other materials to fix the holes in the walls and spent the next five days and nights cleaning, scrubbing, and painting. Unfortunately, my attempts at repairing the walls came out looking terrible. I decided the night before the inspection to give up on the drywall and just pay for it. The rest of the place, though, looked brand-new, with the exception of the first-floor carpets.

Around 3 A.M., a friend from the fraternity, who arrived at my place hammered, asked if I'd drive him back to the dorm. I didn't drink that night. I was high, but I'd never had a problem driving high, so we headed out for the dorm. We made it only a few blocks when my car broke down. I had weed in the car, so the first thing I did was hide it in some nearby ivy. I then called AAA and was told it would be an hour wait for a tow.

Soon after I called AAA, a man in an old Jeep Cherokee pulled over in front of me and asked if I needed help. He said if I didn't want to wait for AAA, he had chains in his car and would be able to tow me back to my place. I was more than happy to take him up on the offer.

He towed me into my garage and unhooked the chains. Just as he was getting back in his car, he noticed the hole in the wall. He told me that he fixed places for a living and offered to help. I said that I was in desperate need of help and there were two other holes that needed to be patched. The inspector was coming at 8 A.M. and it was now four in the morning. I asked him if he could fix the walls right then, and I couldn't believe it when he said he was okay with that. He asked for $40 to finish the whole job.

We went to get his tools, and when we got back to my place, I gave him all the materials to fix the walls. In passing, I asked if he smoked weed and was happy when he said he did. I smoked him down while he fixed my walls. He was a really great down-to-earth guy who finished up the walls by 6 A.M., leaving me two hours to sleep before the inspector came.

When the inspector looked around, he couldn't believe his eyes. He called my place a miracle; at the end of the inspection he told me the only thing that would have to be replaced was the carpet on the first floor. That would cost $500, the exact amount of my security deposit. With five days of hard work and the miracle of my Good Samaritan, I had saved myself $2,000 and the wrath of my dad.

That's the type of luck that I've had my entire life. Over the next few months, however, it began to run out.

-4-
THE GREATEST HONOR EVER

After the townhouse, I moved into a house with
four other guys, including Kyle and a great group of
other housemates. Even though I was surrounded by
positive influences, I became obsessed with smoking
weed. It was all I wanted to do, and it consumed me. I
became less involved at school; my new extracurricular
activity was smoking. I smoked before class and the
first thing after class and at night. I was blowing
through money because I'd become reckless with my
spending when I was high. The $2,000 in loans for that
quarter was gone before I knew it. I soon found myself
asking my mom for money. She questioned me about it,
but I made up a lot of lies about where the money went.
Sphinx

In the winter of my junior year, I received an
email inviting me to Mortarboard, a national senior
class honorary. A friend I knew from the scholars
program told me I should apply for Sphinx instead. She
was a member and said the group accepted only 24
students each year; Sphinx was the oldest honorary on
campus and harder to get into than Mortarboard. Each
member's name was engraved on a plaque next to the
library in Sphinx Plaza. She said I'd meet the best
people at Ohio State and because of the unique bond I'd

have with my class, it was the greatest collegiate experience ever.

My mind was instantly set on getting into Sphinx, so when I got home, I pulled up the application. Writing it turned out to be a great reflection on my college career. I couldn't believe how much I'd been part of in the past three years. The application had to be turned in at a specific day and time; I finished it with just enough time to sprint across the campus. I found out I wasn't alone. There were tons of people rushing to turn in applications, and I hoped mine would hold its own. A couple months went by and I didn't hear anything. I started to lose hope that I had been accepted. On top of that, I had to quit smoking weed because I was trying to get a civil engineering internship. Smoking was my way of dealing with stress, so when I quit I became severely depressed.

ADHD, DEPRESSION, AND ADDERALL

I was having trouble paying attention in class and focusing on studying. I went to the doctor to be tested for ADHD. I took a test and scored a 40; a score of 25 or higher indicates severe ADHD, so I was off the chart and received a prescription for Adderall.

I started to take Adderall at the beginning of spring quarter and it completely changed me. I felt like a zombie, and all I wanted to do was study and be productive. This was not a bad thing in that I got a lot done and had the best grades of my life, but I hated my personality and became increasingly miserable.

The depression lasted for weeks, and I couldn't snap out of it. I called my mom every day, multiple times a day, for some assurance that everything would be okay. She promised me that I had great things to look forward to. There was something she knew that would've brought a huge smile to my face, but she wasn't allowed to tell me about it. It wasn't too long, however, before I found out what she was hiding.

I worked for the Student Wellness Center, and after one of our monthly meetings I set about cleaning the supply closet, which I had promised them I would do for months. I opened up the closet, looked at the mess, and didn't know where to begin. That was when I noticed some students walking towards me in caps and gowns. I thought that they were on their way to see the center's director.

However, they stopped right in front of me. Confused, I asked if I could help them. I'm pretty sure they weren't positive they had the right person, so they looked beyond me to my boss, who was standing there with a camera, and she nodded her head. At that point, one of the guys in a cap and gown pulled out a rolled-up piece of paper. He read off my name and then mentioned all that I was involved with in college. At the end he congratulated me on my linking into Sphinx. Then a blonde girl named Annie linked arms with me, and we walked out of the Student Wellness Center.

I wanted to cry or laugh, but the Adderall made me numb to the situation. In spite of that, right then and there all of my anxieties faded away. I knew that this was a very high honor, but I had no idea what was in store for me that day and just how big an accomplishment this was.

Annie explained to me that I was to remain with my arm linked with hers for the remainder of our journey that day. There were already four others with us that were linked earlier that day. I was the last of the group to be linked, so we headed back to The Oval at the center of the Ohio State campus to meet with the rest of my class.

When we arrived, I noticed that a lot of people from my Sphinx class already knew each other. They were giving each other hugs and congratulations. I kind of felt like the outcast of the group because nobody knew who I was. However, this situation would give me the opportunity to make 23 new friends.

We were lined up for class and individual pictures taken by a professional photographer. A lot of the people had been pulled out of bed, so nobody was really dressed to impress. I was embarrassed by the T-shirt I was wearing because it had a burn hole I'd had gotten from smoking a blunt. I hoped nobody would notice the hole or guess what it was from. I'm pretty sure I was the only one in the class who smoked weed on a regular basis. I didn't want them to find that out.

After having our pictures taken, we lined up at the far end of The Oval where we linked arms with our link. "Carmen Ohio" rang out from the bell tower of Orton Hall. We then took the long walk down The Oval with our link. It was a beautiful spring day, so people all over The Oval were watching us. That walk was a moment I'll never forget. When we got to the far end of The Oval, I was shocked to see my mom, dad, and cousin waiting for me. My mom was crying, and it made me start to tear up a little bit.

We were led past Mirror Lake, an iconic location at Ohio State, to an outdoor amphitheater. Our links walked us in circles around the stage as the announcer read off all that we were involved with in college. It was amazing to hear everyone's story. Although I'd done a lot, it made me question whether or not I fit in with this crowd. But when they called my name and read my accomplishments, I was proud of what I'd done and felt as if I really *did* belong.

The day was filled with more activities, and I received my Sphinx plaque, the most beautiful award I'd ever seen. I was so proud to be one of the 24 chosen that year from my entire class at Ohio State.

After the ceremony, I went back with my family to the house I shared with my friends. My mom told me she had known that I'd been selected for Sphinx for more than a month and that every time I called, crying, she had wanted to tell me so badly. This was more than enough to snap me out of my depression. I was on top of the world.

The organization started to have meetings, and I realized quickly that members of Sphinx were going to be some of the best people I would meet during my college career. They were all very ambitious and driven just like me. They would prove to be an incredible support group for me later that year.

-5-
A SLOW FALL FROM THE TOP

That spring I had a few interviews for civil engineering internships, but I did not land any of the jobs. I decided to move back home for the summer and work with my dad. Self-employed, he fixes heavy industrial machinery. He can fix absolutely anything, and it was amazing to see him at work. I always wanted to see what he did firsthand, and this gave me the opportunity to spend some time with him; that summer we became very close. I loved being with my dad every day because I had not seen enough of him since I left for college.

Nearly every day when I got off work I would practice what I loved most: slalom skiing. This would be my first summer of competition. I had not had this opportunity in the past because before that I was doing show skiing, and the previous summer I taught waterskiing at a summer camp in Maine.

THE CHAMPIONSHIP

My dad had won a state championship in waterskiing in the past and my goal was always to follow in his footsteps. My eyes were set on winning the state championship that summer.

I had access to two great private lakes where I trained and received great coaching, getting myself in shape to be a legitimate contender for the state championship. The fact that these lakes were built specifically for waterskiing was one of the factors that inspired me to change my major from mechanical to civil engineering. When I imagined my dream job, I wanted to focus it around my passion; I decided I wanted to build water-ski lakes. My hope was that one day I would start my own company called "Dream Lakes Construction" and build water-ski lake communities around the country. It didn't hurt that I'd be able to go anywhere in the United States and always have a place to ski.

As I trained that summer, I competed in a few tournaments, and when I got to state tournament, I was seeded second in Ohio. I knew I had a legitimate shot at my dream. No one had ever heard of me, so they had no idea what I was capable of. Most of the people there had been competing since they were young. I met a kid named Ben, who was the top seed for the tournament. This was not just a slalom competition; it was a three-event tournament that also included jump and trick skiing.

For jump, the skier is on two skis, comes up a ramp and jumps. The longest jump wins the competition. Ben said that it was his best event. In trick skiing, the skier is on only one ski that has no fins. Skiers do tricks such as flips and spins and also hold the rope with the feet for toe turns. Ben was also a very talented trick skier. But all I cared about was how good he was at slalom. I asked him what his personal best was, and it was very close to mine. I knew I had a shot. I told him what mine was, but I didn't think he believed me because he had never seen me ski.

The competition began, and I grew more and more anxious awaiting my turn. I listened to my iPod to get myself in the right mindset, and when my turn came for the slalom, I was ready. All my passes around the six-buoy course were going great. I had a final score of 2 1/2 buoys at 32 feet off. This put me in first place, and the only thing standing between me and winning the tournament was Ben.

I swam to shore and watched him run his first few slalom passes with ease, but then he faltered and I knew he had no chance of beating me. I was the Ohio Water Ski Association Men's I State Slalom Champion.

In just one summer I had achieved my dream. I called my dad to tell him the good news. He was so proud of me. Later that day, my coach and I went to the award ceremony, where I was presented with a plaque for first place. On the drive home, I couldn't stop staring at it; I had felt the same way about my Sphinx plaque. I was on top of the world and nothing could bring me down.

That's when the party began.

I worked with my dad for the rest of the summer, but when I got home every day, I immediately went over to a friend's place to get high. We smoked in his basement or, more preferably, we rolled up a blunt and cruised through Franklin Township, which was a nearby rural area.

I thank God I never got caught driving around smoking weed. My 1998 Acura 3.0 CL had dark green mirror tints on it that no one could see through, and we were always very smart about smoking while driving. I kept the windows down and the sunroof open. After we were done smoking, we'd light up a Black and Mild to mask the smell. I spent the rest of the summer like this.

THE BUYING SPREE

When I returned to Columbus to begin autumn quarter at OSU, I realized I had spent everything I made that summer on weed. Because I was receiving tons of junk mail from credit card companies encouraging me to apply for their cards and I wanted some extra spending money, I applied, and soon I had multiple credit cards in my name.

My weed-smoking friend from home came with me to Columbus and took a look at my closet. He said that it would make the perfect grow closet. I was tired of paying for weed, and I also saw this as a way to make some good money. We took a trip to Lowe's, and he showed me everything I needed to start my own hydroponics operation. At a hydroponics store, we bought fertilizer and other things to keep the plants healthy. I bought everything: buckets to put the plants in; lights bulbs; bubblers for an aquarium to keep the water moving; plastic sheeting to cover the walls; and a digital pH tester to make sure the chemicals were mixed properly. I spent more than $600, and my friends from back home helped me to set everything up. When we were finished, I had a professional grow closet, but I still needed plants.

My friend knew a guy in Akron who sold marijuana clones, so he helped me to purchase six Bubblegum Kush clones. Transporting them to Columbus was risky and illegal. I drove very carefully and planted the clones in my closet.

RECKLESS

Now that I had the marijuana growing, all I could think about was the eventual harvest and the profit I would make once I sold it. This thinking got me into a lot of trouble. I applied for more and more credit cards, and I couldn't spend the money fast enough. I decided I wanted a new car. My dream car was a 2004 Laguna Blue BMW M3 convertible. I had no money in the bank, but I figured I could apply for a loan and make payments from the money I made from the plants. I searched online and found the car for $30,000 in Dayton, Ohio.

My friend Ryan and I took the drive to Dayton, where I fell in love with the car right away. I had to have it. I called multiple banks applying for a $30,000 loan, but I was denied every time. Slowly I realized that my dream of taking the car home that day was not going to come true. Over the next few days I kept applying for loans but was continually rejected.

Back in Columbus, I found an older Range Rover for $17,000. Once again I applied for a loan, and once again my request was turned down. The next week, I was back in Akron, and on my way home I drove past a Honda dealership and saw a bright yellow Honda S2000 sitting out front. I stopped at the dealership and told them I was interested in buying the car. The price tag was $36,000, and I applied for a loan. No dice. I was finally starting to realize that I was out of my price range.

THE SEGWAY

When I was back in Stow, I went on a blunt cruise with one of the friends who had helped me set up the grow closet. I told him I was trying to buy a new car but couldn't get financed. He said he knew of something better than a car and that if he had the money, he would buy a Segway. He explained to me how incredible they were and how perfect it would be to get around campus. I would save money on gas and it would stand out more than a BMW. The price tag on a new Segway was $5,000. It just so happened that there was a Segway dealer not far from the campus in Columbus.

I had planned a trip for my Sphinx class to go camping and boating at my folks' place on the Clarion River in Pennsylvania. My car was full of people I barely knew as we headed out for Pennsylvania. I told them that before we left I wanted to stop at the Segway dealer to test one.

Driving one for only a couple of minutes convinced me I had to buy it. I applied in the store for $5,000 in financing but was turned down. I didn't give up.

Instead, I took a trip downtown to the Fifth Third Bank to apply for another loan. My friends from Sphinx couldn't believe how impulsive I was being. They asked me if I should put a little more thought into it, but I was dead set on my decision.

I went into the bank and met with a loan officer. She had no idea what a Segway was and asked if it was like a motorcycle. I said yes and was immediately approved for a motorcycle loan. I walked back to my car with $5,000 in $100 bills. My friends' eyes bugged out in surprise. I took the Segway home in the car with the sunroof open, dropped it off, and then the gang and I were on our way to Pennsylvania. I was eager for the trip to end so that I could get back to Columbus to play with my new toy. Finally I was content with my car, and the Segway was more than enough to make me happy.

This purchase was the beginning of an uncontrolled manic spending spree. I decided that before the summer ended I wanted to go to California. I simply pulled out my credit card and bought a plane ticket. Soon I was on my way.

This journey would be quite an odyssey—and not the best kind.

-6-
HIGH AND HIGHER IN CALIFORNIA

I landed in California in September 2008. Everything was much more beautiful than back home: blue skies, warm temperatures, mountains, and happy people. But all I could think of was where I could find marijuana. The taxi driver took me to Bubblegum Alley—an entire alleyway coated in bubblegum, which was cool and gross at the same time. There I found six people—gay, straight, homeless, fat, hippie, and one in a wheelchair—all willing to share their blunts and pipes. When the pipe came around, I took a hit. It was good shit. I bought some from one of the guys, who was clearly a dealer, while the man in the wheelchair looked out for cops. I came to California for the pot. It did not disappoint.

I listened to the stories of those in the alley: kids kicked out of their homes because they were gay. Kids living on the streets for as little as three weeks and as much as five years. One of the most interesting folks I met was a bum.

"I just got here from New Mexico," he said. "I need to sit down in the grass and get high," the bum said.

"I got what you need. I got weed, hash, mushrooms, crack, cocaine, heroin, whatever," the dealer replied.

"I'll take an eighth of weed."

The dealer weighed it out, passed it to the bum, and left. So did everyone else. It was just me and the bum.

"Want to smoke a joint?" he asked.

As we smoked, he rolled out a few stories. He told me about how he was in Desert Storm. He knew a girl named Marla from New Mexico.

"She was a badass Marine, man. I saw her take on three guys at a bar at one time and then she bought them all beers," he said.

He told me Marla died a few months ago. When her family found out, they came from California and knocked down her house and sold the land. "That's fucked up, man," he said. "So I paid $8,500 for the funeral because I was the only one who cared about her. When I was there, it was only me and the funeral director. I looked at him, and he could tell I wanted to see the body."

He said that once he was left alone with Marla, "I pulled out a joint and pried open her lips. I put the joint in her mouth and lit it. Then I said, 'Burn on, woman!' and closed the coffin."

He shared with me how he would make $190 in an hour-and-a-half by dancing drunk and high in front of a Walmart in New Mexico. "They called me the dancing bum."

When he started telling me about the $2,000 GPS chip in his foot, I decided it was time to move on. Before I left, he told me that if I were to go anywhere in California, I should go to Santa Cruz. It was the weed-smoking capital of the United States.

CALI KIDS

After chilling with the homeless, I met up with a friend from the camp in Maine. The plan for me was to stay at his house for the week, and at one point we were going to go skiing at a lake nearby. But I wanted to see all of California.

I found out that most of his roommates smoked, so I showed off the dank I bought from the homeless guy. It was in a medicine container labeled "Super Purple." They were definitely impressed and ready to try it, so we packed it up and got high. In fact, I stayed high for the entire trip. After all, I was in California, and that's the thing to do there, right? But, to tell the truth, I wasn't any different back in Ohio.

It was late, but all I wanted to do was see the ocean. My friends took me to a state park where we sat on rocks that overlooked the ocean. Although it was dark, it was still a special moment for me to finally see the West Coast.

I sat there drunk and stoned out of my mind, just happily staring at the ocean. The moment was short-lived, though. Suddenly, I heard a loud roar next to me: a sea lion about to attack me. I ran as fast as I could back to the car as the others laughed their asses off. That was when they mentioned to me that the sea lions often came up on the rocks at night to sleep. I could've been killed! Stoners sometimes leave out important details such as giant sea lions. But I laughed it off, and we headed home.

When I woke up the next day, I told my friend I really wanted to travel around California. He agreed with the homeless guy that I should make a trip to Santa Cruz. I bought a Greyhound ticket, packed up my book bag, and left my duffel bag and my ski behind because I figured I'd return to San Luis Obispo later that week.

SANTA CRUZ

I got high for the long trip to Santa Cruz. The scenery was so beautiful, and I was falling in love with California. We were surrounded by mountains and at some points I could see the Pacific Ocean. The sky was blue and the weather was perfect. I was so used to the gray Ohio skies; I had no idea what I'd been missing.

We made a stop a couple hours into the trip, which gave me another opportunity to smoke. A few hours later we arrived in Santa Cruz, and I loved it right away. There were so many cool shops. I needed to be able to cover more ground, so I found a bike shop and purchased the cheapest bike they had for $30. I rode my new bike down to the ocean, passing the most incredible skate park I had ever seen.

Once I got to the ocean, I was blown away. I first came to a pier that had shops on it and extended out to the ocean. I rode to the end of the pier and then took a look around at the beauty surrounding me. The entire area was enclosed by cliffs with gorgeous houses sitting atop them. I dreamed of living up there one day.

To my left was a great beach. I decided that I wanted to go smoke on the cliffs at the far end.

I rode past an amusement park and noticed the sand volleyball courts on the beach. Sand volleyball was one of my favorite hobbies, so this place was heaven to me so far. After carrying my bike down some stairs, I took my first steps in the sand by the Pacific Ocean. I walked up to the base of the cliffs and climbed to the top. When I got there, three kids were already up there smoking weed. I guess I wasn't the only one who thought this would be a sweet smoke spot.

I introduced myself and said I was here from Ohio and that this was my first time seeing the Pacific Ocean in daylight. I pulled out my bottle of "Super Purple" to contribute to the smoke session. I explained that I was there by myself, was just wandering around California, and had no place to stay that night.

After I talked to them for a little while, they asked me if I wanted to stay on their couch. They told me about a website called couchsurfing.org. On this site, people post that they have a couch for someone to sleep on if they want. They said people all over the world offer their couches to travelers. They were part of that site and had gotten great reviews. I trusted them without reviews and took them up on the offer. The only condition they had was that I needed to find some mushrooms and go trip in the redwood forest.

They left, but I stayed on the cliff for a while, staring out over the ocean, reveling in its beauty. I imagined how happy I would be living there one day. I was incredibly at peace sitting there by myself. Eventually I climbed back down the cliff and headed back to town in search of mushrooms. I had tripped only once before, and I really enjoyed it. I thought it would be great to do it in a redwood forest.

As I sat on a park bench watching a homeless man play a guitar, I tried to figure out how I was going to find mushrooms. Then, out of nowhere, a whole band of homeless people showed up. One man played a violin and there was another guy on a banjo. A third man sang, and then other people joined in and started dancing. These were nothing like the homeless people back in Ohio. They had genuine smiles on their faces and they seemed to be very happy. They also all seemed to be drugged out, so asked if anyone knew where I could get mushrooms.

After many failed attempts, I finally ran into a girl who said she could get them for me. However, she wanted to know what she would get in return. I promised her my bike, but when we looked for it, we discovered it had been stolen. To make amends, I gave her some extra cash for the mushrooms. After that, it was off to the bus station for a ride to the forest. I ate the whole eighth of mushrooms at the station before the bus arrived, and during the long ride, they started to hit me. I was dropped off in the middle of nowhere and wandered into the forest. The trees were so beautiful. I had never seen anything like them.

I don't remember too much from that night except having conversations with the trees. They grew faces and started talking to me. I wandered through the forest for about four hours until I finally stopped tripping.

I have no memory of how I got back to the bus stop and made it to my new friends' place, but somehow I did. I knocked on their door and told them about my night, thanking them for their suggestion. We smoked together, and I passed out on the couch.

SAN FRANCISCO

Although I absolutely loved my time in Santa Cruz, I wanted to see the rest of California. I walked to the Greyhound station and grabbed the next bus to San Francisco. The only thing I wanted to see there was the Golden Gate Bridge.

I arrived in San Francisco around 4 P.M. and then spent the rest of the day walking across the city in search of the Golden Gate Bridge. I constantly stopped and asked for directions, and to this day I don't understand why no one told me it was so far away. I got close, but by that time the sun had started to go down. I finally reached the bridge, but it was dark and so foggy that I couldn't see it. I sat on the steps of a building near the bridge and looked over the bay while smoking a Black and Mild.

I could see a lady inside the building, and she noticed me sitting outside on the steps. She must have been sketched out, because eventually the cops showed up. They asked me what I was doing, and I explained to them that I had wandered across the entire city to see the bridge. They told me that I had to leave. Meandering back into the city, I passed a few hotels and stopped in to see what their rates were. Unfortunately, they were so outrageous I decided to stay up for the entire night; I trekked aimlessly throughout the city until the sun came up.

After stopping for breakfast, I found the first marijuana dispensary I had ever seen. I wanted so badly to go inside, but I knew that they wouldn't sell me anything without a medicinal marijuana card. I waited outside the store, and when a guy in his mid-20s came out, I asked him what it was like. He explained the type of stuff they sold; he told me he suffered from chronic pain and that marijuana was the only thing that helped his condition. He showed me a case of energy drinks infused with marijuana he drank every day and offered to give me a couple, which was exactly what I needed.

I drank one of the cans right away. The caffeine

woke me up fast, but it took about 90 minutes for the marijuana to kick in. It was just like eating a weed brownie. I was high out of my mind as I continued to make my way around San Francisco. Just as I was trying to figure out where to go next, I received a phone call that would turn this trip into the best experience of my life.

My friend, Andrei, called to tell me that he and some friends had rented a mansion in the Hollywood Hills for the week of the OSU – USC game. When he invited me to join them, I booked the next flight to Los Angeles.

THE MANSION

While waiting for the plane in San Francisco I gave my friend Grant a call. He'd recently moved from Columbus to Hollywood and offered to pick me up at the airport so he could check out the mansion.

When I arrived, he was driving a Nissan 300ZX, which is one of my all-time favorite cars. But this one was souped up to have more than 400 horse power. As we drove up the winding roads of the Hollywood Hills, the houses became bigger and better the higher we went. I could tell we wouldn't be disappointed when we got to the house where my friends were staying.

Once we arrived, I called Andrei to open the gate. When we passed through, I could see that the house was amazing.

Inside, the place seemed never-ending, and I was astonished by every last inch of it; the murals painted all over the ceilings and walls were stunning. Andrei explained that the guy who repainted the Vatican had been hired to come into the house and paint for two months straight. The murals were the result.

He told me that Paul Oakenfold, one of the nation's leading DJs and remixers, was a neighbor. The homeowners set up a room in the basement with professional DJ equipment so he could DJ parties at the mansion. This was my favorite room in the entire place. We messed around with the equipment and then continued to tour the house. We discovered an Olympic-size pool and hot tub and two giant cabanas, one of which would be my room. The view from the back of the house was breathtaking. The entire pool area was supported on pillars and the balcony below was surrounded by giant bamboo plants. In the past, the mansion had been rented out to shows such as *The Bachelor.* I couldn't imagine what it would cost to rent for a week—and I didn't ask.

All the spending I had done so far had been on credit cards. I went to California with no cash. Literally. For the trip I used cash advances, which, of course, have really high interest rates. But I didn't care about money at all. Surrounded by the people I was staying with, I felt I could spend as much as I wanted.

On my first day, I walked down to Hollywood Boulevard and checked out the stars on the Hollywood Walk of Fame. There were a lot of interesting characters in Hollywood and the people-watching was unmatched. There were guys dressed up like superheroes and other people doing interesting street performances. It seemed like people were trying to make it any way they could.

The street was kind of grungy, with shops on both sides. I came across a smoke shop and ended up swiping my credit card to buy a $300 Roor, which is a top-of-the-line bong. I was eager to test it, so I took it back to Grant's apartment and put it to good use. Loved it.

Later that day, Grant and I happened into some shops, including the Apple Store. I came across the MacBook Air, which had just been released. It was so light and thin compared to my old laptop, and I almost bought it on the spot. On the ride home, all I could think about was that laptop, but there was a $1700 price tag. As a bonus, it came with an iPod Touch.

By the time we made it back to the apartment, I decided to buy the computer. After a short conversation with the credit card company, my credit limit was raised, and I was ready to make the purchase. I even paid extra for the overnight shipping to make sure I got it before I left California.

I spent my entire trip in California swiping away as if there were no limit to the amount of money I had. I bought a pair of Bose headphones to go along with the iPod Touch. Since I was living out of a book bag and all of my clothes were in San Luis Obispo, I bought an entire new wardrobe. All I could think was that I had those plants at home; as soon as they were done growing, the money would come.

As Grant drove me throughout Los Angeles, I loved his car more and more. I told him I was willing to buy it. Eventually, I spent a day looking for loans for $10,000 so I could have the car. I pictured myself driving it back to Ohio. That day would never come because I never got a loan approved.

My spending was out of control and I couldn't help myself. I was surrounded by wealth. I told myself that one day I would have a lot of money, so it didn't matter what I spent.

Grant took me to Malibu, where we took a walk on the beach. As we ambled along, we ran into a couple with their son. I stopped to talk to them and noticed a bowl sitting next to them. I asked them if I could smoke with them. Their son was playing in the sand; they said his name was Marley, after Bob Marley. This kid was five years old and had dreadlocks down to his shoulders. He was wearing a tie-dye Bob Marley T-shirt. This was definitely the coolest-looking kid I had ever seen.

I had never swum in the Pacific Ocean so I ran and dived into the waves. The water was freezing, even though it was the end of summer. The summer before, I had had a picture taken of me in Maine on some rocks out in the Atlantic Ocean. I had my arms out to my side with my palms facing up posing like I was a king. On the beach in Malibu was a rocky spot just like it. I had Grant take a picture of me in the same pose, but this time on the other side of the country.

As we walked back down the beach, Grant started laughing and pointed out the couple we had met earlier. The two of them were having sex right in the middle of the beach. There was about a four-foot drop-off on the beach that made a wall for us to hide behind. We peeked over the wall and laughed as we watched them go at it. I then looked over and noticed that they had left Marley playing in the sand by himself. Not the greatest parenting.

The night before the Ohio State – USC game was a huge party at the mansion catered by Nobu—the world's most-recognized Japanese restaurant. In the words of Kate Winslet, Nobu is "heaven on earth and sex on a plate." Just to cater appetizers was $500 a head, and there had to be at least 50 people at the party. The open bar featured a lychee and elderflower martini, which was the best drink ever. I couldn't get enough of them. One of the people renting the house also brought probably 20 bottles of Cristal. I found myself double-fisting the martinis and the Cristal. I definitely was not the classiest person at this party. Andrei was in a similar state, and about halfway through the party the host told us we probably should go to a club.

On Game Day I woke up early, rolled a blunt, lit it up, and took a walk down the streets of the Hollywood Hills. I stared at the beautiful houses and dreamed of success. Heading back to the mansion, I found everyone was getting ready for the game. Eventually a stretch black Lincoln Navigator limousine pulled up to take us to the stadium. The only time I had been in a limo was for my senior prom, but this limo blew that one away. It was stocked with top-shelf liquor, and on the way we picked up a ton of appetizers for the ride. On top of that, one of the guys had a box of the number two cigars in the world; we lit those up on the way.

When we arrived at the Los Angeles Memorial Coliseum, we found our way to a huge tailgate that was just for Ohio State fans. There was a victory rally with members of the "Best Damn Band in the Land" and prominent speakers from Ohio State. Because I hadn't packed any Ohio State memorabilia, I bought a T-shirt that said 'FUSC' on it. At the game, we were surrounded by Ohio State fans who had traveled across the country just to see this game. USC got off to a hot start and never stopped. Silencing the thousands of

Ohio State fans, they humiliated OSU with a final score of 35 to 3.

We spent our last night at the mansion, and the next morning it was time to head back to Ohio. The only problem was that my ski and the rest of my stuff were still in San Luis Obispo. After another Greyhound trip, I met up with my friends, who couldn't believe the stories I told them about my California adventures. Later that day, I booked my flight to Columbus.

It was Sunday. Classes were to start the next day, but I wasn't ready for the party to end.

-7-
SPIRALING

I landed in Columbus and went to my classes to pick up the syllabi and attend the first lectures. But I didn't learn much that quarter. I didn't go to class. I had my Segway to ride all over the city, and I still had a pretty hefty credit line to play with.

Just a few days into the quarter, I got sick. The doctor said it was a very bad sinus infection and prescribed medication that included codeine. A visiting friend—the one who helped me set up my closet—convinced me to take extra doses, and I began to feel *way* too good. He then told me that it was even better to roll blunts in the medicine. I tried that and was higher than I had been in my life. I had no idea how addictive codeine is, and I continued to just crave more.

By the second day we'd gone through the entire bottle. I even cut it in half so I could scrape the bottom with a cotton swab and get every last drop. I rubbed it on my gums as if it were cocaine. I was desperate to keep the high going. I called the doctor and said I'd spilled the bottle, and needed a refill. She said she normally would not re-prescribe, but she did it this once.

When we got the next bottle, my friend showed me how to make "purple drank," a mixture of codeine, lemon-lime soda and hard candies. We split the bottle of codeine in half and poured it into bottles containing the other ingredients. We then drank both bottles. I got even higher than I'd been before, and the pattern persisted for several days.

After going through my codeine binge, I didn't care what drugs I did. I wanted to experiment with everything and didn't give a thought to my mental health. My roommates were becoming very concerned; they also didn't like my drugged-up friend, who carried a gun in the waistband of his sweatpants. Meanwhile, I found my way to painkillers such as Percocet and Vicodin, shut out reality, and did things I never would have done if I hadn't been on drugs.

I took out a $1,200 cash advance so I could buy a pound of weed for my friend to sell; we were supposed to split the profit. He sold the first pound and then told me that there was no profit. Although I had smoked a good deal of it, it was hard to believe that there was no profit at all. He used the money he made to buy another pound and sold that. Once again there was no profit. I found out later that the profit probably was going straight into his arm because he was a heroin addict.

I didn't learn my lesson. I took out another $400 for a quarter-pound of weed that was fronted to me by a guy I'd met only once. My plan was to deliver it to my friend to sell the next weekend. That never happened.

A new high

The next day, a friend of mine from the water ski team came over with two others friends and suggested we try acid. I was hesitant at first, but they told me they'd dropped it about 40 times over the summer. I decided to give it a shot. We each took two hits.

Because it would take about 90 minutes for the acid to hit, we decided to get out of the house. I rode my Segway; when I got to High Street (ironic, isn't it?), the acid kicked in. I felt as if I were inside the Segway trying to figure out its inner workings. It blew my mind. The ride back to my house, which took about five minutes, felt like an eternity.

When I got home, some neighbors sitting outside realized I was messed up, and they took things a little further. One of them had a gun, and when I said I was tripping on acid, he pointed the gun at me, moving it back and forth very fast. I was sure he was going to accidentally shoot me, so I ran inside. I locked every door and window, closed the blinds, and curled up on the couch in the fetal position, scared for my life.

Eventually the fear subsided and the friends I'd been tripping with came home. I decided that we should smoke some of the weed I'd bought. I rolled blunt after blunt after blunt.

An acid trip comes in waves. It will get very intense and then levels off. It feels as if it's over, but it comes back with a vengeance. The trip lasted about 13 hours, and for most of that time we rolled blunts and smoked them. In one night, the four of us people smoked the entire quarter-pound of weed. After that, I slept for an entire day.

When I woke up, it was to the realizations that we'd smoked everything, and I now owed $400 to a guy I didn't even know. I had spent so much money I could no longer get a cash advance to pay him back. The credit card companies were now unwilling to raise my credit limit.

The dealer who fronted me the weed gave me a call a few days later looking for his money. I explained to him that I needed a bit more time. When the allotted time passed, I received a call threatening me if I did not get the money up. I finally offered the dealer my Xbox 360 and Grand Theft Auto IV, with a little money to follow. He was furious but he agreed to the proposition.

My binge continued with a drunken, drugged-out trip with the waterski team to Lake Norris. I drank enormous amounts of beer; cadged, begged, and pleaded for Vicodin from a friend who had a bad ankle sprain; and tried to steal more from another member of the group. After she caught me, I realized I had a problem with painkillers, and I never took another. The trip ended with an accident that could have been fatal based on the amount of alcohol everyone had on board.

It was now three weeks into the quarter, and I still hadn't been to class. Exams were about to begin and I wasn't prepared. I sent a lying email to my professors saying that my sinus infection had progressed to pneumonia, and they allowed me to make up the exams when I felt better. Feeling better was a long time coming.

Cocaine

As I was recovering from my "pneumonia," a friend invited me over to his place to try cocaine. I wasn't sure I wanted to, but I had snorted Adderall in the past, so it wasn't the first time something had gone up my nose. I took both lines of cocaine and the effect was very quick. I was energetic and euphoric. It felt like Adderall, but much stronger. I called all my friends, talking a thousand miles a minute. As the effects wore off, I craved more, but my friend couldn't lay his hands on any. Euphoria became irritability, and that was a turning point for me. I knew somehow that I was reaching rock bottom. I had to make changes.

The next day, a Friday, I emailed one of my professors that I was ready to make up my exam. It was scheduled for Monday, giving me three full days to study four weeks' worth of material in my hardest engineering class.

On Sunday, I woke up with a terrible hangover from a party the previous night. I called around trying to score a few Adderall so I could do some intensive cramming. I eventually found two of the strongest dosages available, went to my cousin's house in the suburbs, and began to study about 10 P.M. for an early-morning exam. Arriving back on campus, I started the exam in the TA's office. My mind went blank. I had memorized a list of equations, but they were slipping away. I knew how to do the problems, but couldn't without the equations. I persuaded the TA to help me because I'd just come off weeks on pneumonia and had only three days to study. As it turned out, I actually did all right on the test, but the end was coming.

-8-
CRASHING

The day before my entry into the hospital, I spent part of the afternoon at my house smoking with some of my friends, and I was gripped by euphoria once again. I was extremely talkative, but no one noticed because no one was listening. I went into another room and found Kyle studying. With the Adderall wearing off, reality was setting in. I thought about all the drugs I had done, how far behind I was in my classwork, and how much money I had spent.

Looking around the room, I was astounded at what I'd bought: a $5,000 Segway; a MacBook Air; an iPod Touch; a huge computer screen to hook up to my laptop; a wireless keyboard so I could veg out in my bed and mess around on my computer; the $600 worth of hydroponics gear for my grow operation; and other random electronics, along with a whole new wardrobe.

I didn't know how much I'd spent, but I knew the number would be huge. Checking a credit report site, I was stunned to discover I'd spent more than $15,000 in two months and applied for nearly 40 loans and credit cards. I had missed payment after payment and there was no way I could grow enough weed to pay it off.

The plants were stressing me out more and more. I'd showed them off to too many people, and I felt as if the police were going to knock on the door at any moment. I became more and more paranoid. I wanted to get rid of the plants. My older brother knew about them and urged me to destroy them. I still thought they were the answer to my debt problems, though, so I wasn't ready to let them go.

I made a list of all the things I had to do to get myself back on track. It was never-ending and overwhelming. Seeing on paper what I had to do only added to the stress. I went through the items one by one, but eventually I realized it was too much for me to handle. I had to come clean to my parents and turn myself in. I needed all the help I could get. Kyle thought it was a good idea for me to go to my parents. After I talked with him, I wrote him an email that listed the things I was stressing about. Part of the letter read:

> "I can't stop freaking out
> about everything. Just
> make time to talk with me
> tomorrow. Let's go
> somewhere. Let's get
> away from campus. I
> want to go over
> everything I have been
> doing wrong. I mean I
> know there has to be
> more positives but I want
> to make some serious
> changes. I want to be a
> role model again. I want
> to live up to why my
> niece calls me her hero ...
> Jesus ... I need sleep.

You know when I stress I
have a hard time
stopping. I need to talk to
you. It's just a bunch of
little things or big things.
I think it's just hard for
you to understand
because you don't have
this problem really. But
here's a list:

- Coke, weed, shit in closet, dad,
  sloppiness, slacking, ski team
- Credit card debt. I honestly want to
  cry. You all told me how fucking stupid
  I am, and now I'm right here. Collectors
  call all day long. I'm freaking out. I need
  to figure something out. I need access to
  eBay but I don't want to ask my mom for
  a credit card. I really need help
  financially because this really is freaking
  me the fuck out.
- Here it is ... These are just some of the
  payments I can think of:
    - Electric. Still need to pay $330.
      It was due on the 10th. For some
      reason I am very scared to ask
      my parents for money. Mainly
      because my mom showed me a
      list of everything she's given me,
      over $2,300, over the summer for
      random stuff.
    - Citicard. Missed last 2

payments. $39 fees...

- 5/3 credit card. $500 payment due at the end of month.
- Segway. Missed $170 payment... Didn't even check the fee.
- My bank. Fraud screwed up everything. I lied about the amount. It was over $400. I had like $300 in my bank. Then a ton of transactions went through. I checked over the last week it was like -$50 to -$100 to -$300. I'm scared to check. I need to go to the bank. I got a call from Blockbuster today saying that I was charged for Grand Theft Auto IV. Oh, God, I just realized that I never returned a movie to North Campus Video. My card is on file.
- TJMaxx. Never paid that off.
- Walmart. Haven't looked at statement.
- Lowe's. Probably owe about $15 and it's probably fucking me.

Obviously I need serious help. Please dude, tomorrow just make this a priority. I need you more than ever. I know that I'll be all right. I do need sleep but this is really hard to sleep on."

The next day, a Wednesday, I wrote a 13-page email to my family, laying out everything about the drugs and spending problems. I ended by saying:

> "My mind is clear and it really has never been this clear in my entire life. I finally have a good head on my shoulders again. I promise to all of you that I'm going to change drastically. I'm going to fix everything on this list I've created. I currently have 42 items written down. I have been crossing things off all day. I have created major goals for myself. I had already started to prioritize them. I will keep you posted as to what I accomplish. I love you all!"

That night I still could not sleep. I hadn't slept since Saturday night and it was now Thursday morning. I was really starting to lose it. That morning I got a call from Mom. She was sobbing and said that she called off work for the next two days so she could come and take me home. I begged her to let me try and fix the situation myself, but she knew I was in over my head. A couple of hours later she arrived in Columbus. She gave me a big hug and cried some more.

My mom had called my dad and explained to him what I had written to her. He was furious about the situation and started to holler at me. I broke down crying and didn't know what to say. I told him that I was going to fix it and I was going to change. My Dad was so disappointed in me, and I was heartbroken. I was starting to realize more and more how much I had screwed up.

My mom took me away from campus to my cousin's place. I was right where I needed to be, which was with family. I was finally starting to feel at ease. I knew they would help me, but I think if I had waited one more day I would have been so far gone I would never have been able to climb out of the hole I was in. I finally slept a little. All it took was the comfort of my mom's hand on my back to let me sleep.

-9-
A CRAZY DAY

My cousin read the letter I wrote my mom, and she told me to drop all my classes. We were dealing with something much more serious, and school could wait. My mom made the phone call to the university, and I called the Student Wellness Center to let them know I wouldn't be reporting to work for at least the rest of the quarter. The people who worked there really cared about me and they were definitely concerned. I told them there was nothing to worry about and I'd be back soon.

TEARING DOWN THE CLOSET

Once we took care of all the administrative business, we went back to my house and destroyed the grow closet. I pulled the plants, threw them into the bathtub and shredded them until they were just a green mess. I poured chemicals on them, put them into multiple trash bags and threw them into the dumpster down the alley.

Destroying those plants lifted a massive weight off my shoulders. I continued to disassemble the grow closet. What did continue to worry me was the massive amount of debt I had accumulated. I was thinking of any possible way to make a dollar. The plants were supposed to pay for most of the debt, but now they were gone.

I didn't want to throw away the $600 I'd spent on lights, buckets, chemicals, and pumps. These could be sold now that the plants were gone. There is nothing illegal about a hydroponics set up without the weed. My mom failed to agree. She wanted it all to be gone, and when she found out I had hid it all down in the basement she made me go down and throw it out. Everything was gone and for once I felt free of it.

But my breakdown was in full force. Three hours of sleep in nearly five days made me psychotic. Suddenly everything became a special sign. The title of every single book on my desk, the song on the radio, the weather, a picture. Everything had meaning, and these signs were so obvious I couldn't believe I was the only one who saw them.

Something led me to believe that the rain outside was going to stop at a certain point at a song I was listening to. I went to tell my roommate, who was definitely concerned. He had been for weeks, but this was a different level of craziness. I continued to stare out the window waiting for the rain to instantly stop.

My mom came up the steps and saw me standing there with a stack of books. I was waiting for her so that I could explain the signs to her. When it came time to explain the meaning of the book *Rich Dad, Poor Dad*, I brought her to tears. The rich dad was my uncle, my dad's oldest brother. He retired at 50 and had been living in Florida for more than 20 years. My father was the poor dad. He was 63 and far from retiring. I explained to my mom that I knew we were going through some financial troubles, but we were going to be okay. She just had to have confidence in me and my twin brother, Aaron. We were going to graduate from college soon, and we were going to be able to help them get through it all. I said Dad should retire. When she didn't agree, I became upset and raised my voice at her. She was in tears and kept repeating, "This is not Adam. This is not you!" She left the house crying and went for a walk down the street. I continued to clean up the mess.

SIGNS FROM GOD

Later, Mom came back upstairs and helped me finish packing. I think she had told herself to ignore the crazy stuff and just get me back home. By the time we got into the car, I was starting to lose it altogether. My mom had no idea that I had an entire box full of random items I thought were signs from God. I took the box home so I could explain the signs to my family.

About halfway home, the signs from God got a little out of control. Everything was a sign at this point. Even the street signs and the billboards off of the highway were signs. It was a two-hour drive from Columbus to Stow, but it felt like the longest two hours of my life. It must have felt like an eternity for my mother. When we got home, my Dad was waiting on the couch for us. My mom had already warned him that it was not me. Then out came the box.

I told my parents there were some things that I wanted to show them. One by one I went through the box of items and explained them to my parents. The delusion that I was Jesus was taking hold. I said that all our troubles were going to disappear, we would have all the money in the world, and we would move to

Hollywood and live in the mansion I stayed in during my trip.

I even told them that I was going to die in 2012. That 2012 was not the end of the world, but it was the date of my death. But until the day of my death, our lives were going to be incredible. Once I died, there would be complete world peace, and we would always be happy. For obvious reasons, these ramblings scared the hell out of my parents.

I thought I was doing them a favor by sharing the signs. They should be happy to hear these things from me. Eventually, I got so upset no one would believe me that I went to my room to be alone. They would not leave me alone, though, because I was so far gone. This made me angry and my heart raced. My parents called 9-1-1.

My brother talked to me to calm me down. He knew that bringing drama to the situation would only make my heart beat faster. I screamed at him to turn off the light. I needed to turn off every sound and every light around me to slow my heart. He turned off the light and sat there with me quietly, and my heart rhythm returned to normal.

For some reason, I believed that turning off the light saved me. I thought if it had stayed on for one more second, my heart would have exploded inside my chest. It was then I remembered a story my dad had told me about a schizophrenic man who tried to get rid of the voices that spoke to him by smashing a light bulb on his forehead—to actually burn the voices out of his head. When the light turned off, I was sure my life had been saved. Right then and there, I knew I had solved the mystery of schizophrenia. All anyone had to do was turn off the light. My mind drifted further and further from reality.

All the signs had to mean something. Maybe it was something greater? The delusions of grandeur took over, but by this time I could see the light from the ambulance coming to get me.

I told the first responders to stop and listen to me. I went on to explain: "You are all about to be a part of history! I am Jesus Christ and I'm here to help you!"

TO THE HOSPITAL

I had a copy of the Bible still in my hand and I started to go through it with them. "The New Testament. Crap! The Old Testament. Truth!" Eventually my parents stepped in and pulled me away from them, saying they'd take me to the hospital themselves. We all piled into our Chevy Tahoe, and as we drove off I moved more and more toward insanity.

When we arrived at the hospital, I thought that I owned the place. As the Son of God, I was pretty sure I had a tremendous amount of power. No doctor or nurse was going to tell me otherwise. As my parents talked with the doctors, I waited in an intake room at the Emergency Department. The guy who was observing me was some scrawny male nursing student. It was Jesus versus a confused kid, and I was about to own his world.

There was nothing in the room that I could really mess around with. I looked at a valve marked oxygen and laughed while pressing every button and switch I could find. "My father invented oxygen," I said. The nurse told me to sit down. Then I found the pull string for the emergency call button. Fuck it. I pulled it. An alarm went off and more nurses rushed to my room. My nurse told them it was okay. As soon as they left, it was time to sound the alarm once more. The nurses came back and demanded that I do not do it again.

Eventually they took me to the MRI area to see how far gone I really was. When I returned to my room, it was just the male nurse and me again. The kid came off as gay, so I talked to him about that. The fact that I was Jesus Christ and thought it was okay to be gay meant that he would be all right. I thought he'd appreciate my support, but he just said he wasn't gay. When another nurse came to administer a drug test, my male nurse had enough of me. He stormed out, and I failed the drug test.

The nurse said there were so many drugs in my system she couldn't believe I was still alive. This statement fed my fantasy of being immortal. I vaguely remember being moved down a hall. I was in God's hands now and this was just all part of the plan. It would be some time before I was ready to face the world again.

-10-
THE WARD

THE FIRST DAY

After waking in my room with "Kyle," I walked down the hall and into the main area, which had a kitchen with some tables, a game area, and a waiting room with a television.

As I circled the room, I was sure God still was laying out my every step by giving me very obvious signs. I only had to figure them out, so I looked for them everywhere. I came upon a wall phone surrounded by phone numbers written in pencil, and I was sure the numbers were a sign. I had once seen an episode of *South Park* in which Towelie, a talking towel engineered by crazy scientists to be some type of weapon, is trying to remember the code to get into a government base. He plays random numbers on a security keypad until he comes across the beat to "Funkytown," and yells out, "I got it!"

So, among all the numbers penciled by that wall phone, I tried to find the ones that would give me the beat to "Funkytown." I kept hitting the numbers on the telephone keypad, but after trying countless combinations that didn't work, I finally gave up.

By the way, Towelie also smoked a lot of weed, and his signature catchphrase was, "Want to get high?"

Before entering the psych ward, my life was somewhat like his—and far too often.

Once I finished trying to find the magical "Funkytown" beat, I was called to a meeting by a lady named Kathy. She went over the daily activities that were scheduled, along with visiting hour times and what we could choose for breakfast, lunch, and dinner. We were given a small list of menu items to choose from, but, to me, even the menu seemed to be to be some kind of challenge or code. I thought there must be a correct answer. I carefully selected a few things, ordering the same items again for the next few days because I swore there was some message buried in the menu. I ordered tomatoes on my cheeseburgers, even though I absolutely hate tomatoes.

I finally turned in my menu, which gave me some time to think about what was going on. As I came to the understanding that I was in a psych ward, it made perfect sense to me. Jesus locked up with all the crazies? Why not? After all, Jesus was thought to be so crazy in his previous life that they nailed him to a cross. The psych ward was the perfect place for Jesus to be. I was safe from everyone else here. I was on lockdown and under watch 24 hours a day, and I was on every television screen in the world. The Christians had been right all along, and now they were protecting their prophet.

As I walked around the rest of the ward, I saw more and more people I knew. They were friends from the leadership program at Ohio State, but they all looked a little different. Like my roommate, they'd been dressed and made up like actors. Could all of my friends really just be actors? I thought my life was just like *The Truman Show*. The cameras must have been on me for a long time. My entire life had all been documented. These actors, who I thought were my friends, had cameras and other technology to capture evidence. This was the age when they could prove Jesus was real.

I grew tired of saying I was Jesus, so I dropped the name and just went on with the act. I even called the people around me by the names of my friends—the people I thought they really were. I totally messed with their heads.

When I got back to my room, I saw a few magazines lying on the nightstand. Grabbing some entertainment magazines—*People* and *US*—I started searching for clues. They were everywhere in news magazines. I pulled out key phrases and gave them meaning.

THE ESCAPE

After I'd been on lockdown for a week and hadn't seen the outdoors, my number one priority was getting out of the ward. I waited for the day when the entire world would get to meet me. I was sure there was something I was supposed to do, but I couldn't figure it out. I continued my search for signs all day every day, but nothing ever happened.

I spent each day waiting for something significant to happen. The hospital's helicopter pad was right outside of my window, and every time it flew by I prayed it was coming for me.

After a while, though, I became furious. I wanted answers about why I was locked up. I refused to believe that drugs were the reason or that I had any kind of problem. No one would believe me when I told them that I was Jesus Christ. I had to get out of there. Escape was essential.

I checked every single window on the entire floor. I peeked into all of the other patient's rooms and looked for windows and doors to get out of. I couldn't find one. Then it came to me. The only way to get out was to get the keys. That shouldn't be too hard. After all, the people on the floor weren't prison guards; they were nurses who were mostly middle-aged women.

I knew the hospital had cameras and that security was most definitely watching what was going on, but since I was Jesus Christ I really had nothing to lose.

Sitting at a table near the kitchen, I looked around at all of the nurses. To my relief, I noticed that their keys were clipped directly to their belt loops. All I had to do was grab them. A nurse came by to put away some food in the fridge, which was locked up. She had to use her keys to open it, and as soon as she went for them, I tried to jerk them away. She saw me at the last second, put her keys away, and walked off.

Frustrated, I made an attempt to snatch another nurse's keys. She noticed me coming at her, ran into an office, and pulled an alarm. All of a sudden the entire staff was after me. Looking down the hallway, I saw a janitor walking out the door. I raced for the open door, but I was too late. Screwed for sure.

When I turned around, a monster of a woman was standing there ready to set me straight.
"I have two sons that are about three times your size and I can take them both to the ground," she said. "I'm not going to have any problem with you!"

Trying to run away from her wasn't a smart move. Pretty soon it seemed as if the entire staff was dragging me to my room.

I looked at the barred windows and decided to throw a fit. I wanted to know why I was here and why this was all happening to me. I was feeling a thousand emotions at once and didn't know what to do with myself.

My choice wasn't a good one. I heaved a heavy wooden desk chair across the room at the metal screen over the window. I threw it so hard that it bounced all the way back to me.

The next thing I knew I was pinned to the bed and the staff members holding me down appeared to be waiting for something. That something was a giant hypodermic needle heading right for my ass. Just as someone was about to jam it into my butt cheek I cried out, "Rape! Why would you put that in my ass? It hurts!" I thought the television viewers would get a laugh out of that one. Maybe I wasn't setting the best example for the kids, but Jesus saying that would be pretty funny to me.

The fun didn't end there. Big Bertha dragged me to the isolation room. At this point I knew I'd really screwed up. Out of the entire psych ward, I was the craziest. The winner for the day. Bertha threw me into the room and told me to behave myself. I didn't have much choice because the drugs were knocking me out.

When I woke up, I walked around the room and tried to find a way out. The entire room was painted white and there were no windows, with the exception of a small one in the door for the staff to look through.

I had never felt so helpless. Without a magazine or a window, I couldn't receive any signs. With a calmer mind, I realized that if I wanted to get out of isolation, I had to behave myself.

I sat there for a few hours until I was able to convince the nurse I was ready to do that. She agreed to let me go back to my room and go to sleep if I gave her my clothes. I would have to earn them back. For the next few days, I wore only a hospital gown and my boxers underneath. It took me three days to earn my clothes. Three days of hard work.

THE SIGNS KEEP COMING

As I've indicated, my life in the ward was driven by signs. I could take anything and give it some kind of symbolic meaning. I got my signs from the people that I interacted with, the artwork the patients made, shampoo bottles, toothpaste, ketchup packets, and anything else sitting around.

I remember reading antiperspirant and breaking the word down until it became that it was "anti-spirit." That sign told me that wearing deodorant would make the signs harder to read; I would lose my powers.

During art therapy one day, I drew my name—Adam Christopher Helbling—and then proceeded to break it down. Adam was the first man on earth, as it says in the Bible. Christopher was for Christ. I drew the Christ portion of my name very large because I thought this further proved that I was Jesus Christ.

I don't remember every sign, of course, but some of them stand out. When I was allowed to make phone calls from the public phone, I called Kyle—the real one. I wanted him to tell me that the idea of my being the Second Coming was true, but what he said instead was that I had to persevere to get through this difficult experience. He said it over and over until it was drilled into my head.

When I hung up, I glanced at a magazine about horses. An article in the magazine was titled 'Perseverance.' It explained that winning racehorses had a certain rhythm in their steps: a 1-2-3, 1-2-3, 1-2-3 pattern. I put down the magazine and started walking up and down the hallways like a racehorse. I repeated the pattern in my head as I stepped. For the next few days, I walked the halls counting out, "1-2-3, 1-2-3, 1-2-3." I thought that was the way I was supposed to walk, but I'm sure that was far from what Kyle had in mind when he suggested perseverance.

Another elaborate sign came when I was taking a shower. The hot water felt great. As I rinsed my hair, I opened my eyes and started to laugh. I thought the shower nozzle looked like a penis, and I translated this to mean that God was taking a piss on me to wash off all the filth and mistakes I had made in my life. It was like God's penis had just baptized me again. After I finished my shower, I felt like a new man.

A moment later, I noticed that my feet were still submerged in water. The drain was clogged. I thought it meant that God had washed off so much filth that it couldn't fit down the drain. I realized that the shower was just like the shower in my dorm from my freshman year—the one I used to let fill up to the top of the lip so I could take a bath and vomit in the toilet at the same time. The water in this shower was right up to the top of that lip, too. I was sure this was a sign reminding me of how screwed up I used to be and that I should never get that way again.

That night, I went to wash my hands for dinner and was overcome by a strange obsession. I ran my right hand under the water once and then my left hand and then my right hand again. I started to think there was something holy about the number three and doing things three times. So as I ran each hand through the water I would say, "In the name of the Father, the Son, and the Holy Spirit." From that day on I did it every time I washed my hands, and the hand washing became more and more frequent.

Because I was Jesus, I had little regard for rules, and I was afraid of nothing. I constantly pulled the red emergency cords. This drove the nurses to distraction, but they finally began to disregard the alarms.

Although I was a handful, I knew that Jesus would help people, and I thought that was important for me to do. Even though I wasn't allowed to enter other patient's rooms, I did it, and I talked to them. I tried to heal them as if I had magical Jesus powers. They would talk about the voices in their heads, the drugs they did, or even why they tried to kill themselves.

One day a suicidal young woman broke down in front of me. The nurses took her away to try to calm her down. While she was away, I quickly wrote her a letter about how much she had to live for. She constantly wrote a journal; I read a great deal of it and was very impressed. I wrote that she should write a book because she could help people who felt the same way she did and might prevent them from taking their own lives. She was so thankful for the letter. I felt great to be able to help someone in need. Later she sent me a Facebook message that she was writing her book.

In spite of my good works, the nurses were always chasing me back to my room.

ON THE OTHER SIDE

The psych ward had two units. The first was for those people who legally should've been locked up. Like me. There was a police order for me to stay there until released by a psychiatrist. The other unit was called stress management and was for those people who were on their way out.

When I was on the crazy side, the staff constantly talked about how my goal was to get to the other side. This only messed with my head because I thought that crossing over to the other side was like crossing over to heaven. But since I was still on Earth, I thought it meant that the place would be heaven on Earth. Jesus was back and we were about to experience world peace. When the day came for me to go to the other side, I thought it meant that my time had come. However, the only difference was that the refrigerator wasn't locked up and we had access to all the sandwiches and juice we could eat and drink.

On the crazy side, the number of visitors was limited. On the stress management side, I could have my entire family visit at once. The first night they came to see me, I was overwhelmed. My sister was wearing a cross. I complimented her. I thought she was saying she knew who I was.

My family knew I was still far from my normal self. My dad went out in the hallway and broke down crying. My sister later told me it was the first time she had ever seen my dad cry. I, on the other hand, was excited, thinking that my family was finally going to take me home.

The television was on and an episode of *60 Minutes* was starting. I watched as the correspondents were introduced. I anticipated that the show was going to be about the Second Coming of Jesus Christ. The whole world had been watching me for weeks now and it was finally time for me to meet the world. When they introduced the topics for the evening, I was disappointed and stormed out of the room. When was I going to leave this place?

I went into the lobby area, where I found a cell phone on a table. I put the phone to my ear, waiting for my instructions about what I was to do next. The man whose phone it was chased me down the hall and grabbed it back, looking at me as if I were insane.

The next thing I knew, I was running from nurses who took me back to the crazy side, away from my family. Now it was going to take even longer to get out.

FINALLY GOING HOME

I spent a few days on the crazy side until I was sent back to stress management.
There I met with a psychiatrist to get my medications straightened out. For the first week or so, I was completely against taking my medications. I didn't think Jesus needed to be on medication. As I took the medications regularly, however, the signs slowly faded away.

During this period, one particular phone call really helped. I told an ex-girlfriend about all the signs I was receiving. She said that maybe the signs were not telling me that I *was* Jesus. Maybe the signs were telling me that Jesus was there to *help*. What she said changed everything. I realized that maybe God was talking to me because I needed His help.

As the signs disappeared, I was able to tell my psychiatrist that I no longer believed I was Jesus. This was the biggest step in getting out of there. My family was so relieved to see that I had my sanity back. However, the fight was still far from over.

A male nurse who was working on the stress management floor told me about delusions of grandeur. He told me that nine times out of 10, when people think they are a greater being, that being is Jesus. There were times on the ward when he saw two people believe that they were Jesus. They would constantly argue over who was the actual chosen one.

I was released on Election Day 2008—the McCain-Obama election. Right before I left, an obese lady on the floor came up to me and said that the voices in her head were telling her McCain was going to win. I left with my mother thanking God that I was no longer in that state of mind.

-11-
CLEAN . . . ALMOST

REHAB

The psych ward was only the first part of my recovery. I started in a partial rehabilitation program a few days after my release. Sessions ran from 9 A.M. until 3:30 P.M. Monday through Friday. We had group therapy throughout the day led by several different psychologists. Each day, we met with the psychiatrist to explain how we were doing. We also took part in art therapy. This program helped me learn to deal with stress in a positive way.

When I met with my psychiatrist, he explained to me that I had bipolar disorder; I had just gone through a manic episode and a psychotic break. To keep it from happening again, I had to take my medications and stay drug- and alcohol-free. Because I was living at home with my parents, this part of the program was easy. The test would come when I returned to Ohio State in the spring.

I really enjoyed the group therapy sessions. We were all in it together and we supported and encouraged one another. It was helpful to hear the others' various problems because it made mine seem not so big.

I spent three-and-a-half weeks in the partial rehabilitation program, learning how to cope with stress without smoking marijuana. After my time in the partial program, I was sent to a rehab program for drugs. I spent two-and-a-half weeks in that program. This one wasn't as helpful. Most of the people in my group were middle-aged women addicted to painkillers. Others were addicted to heroin and other harder drugs. I felt as if they focused too much on alcohol dependence and talked very little about the dangers of marijuana. I came out still believing that weed was not a dangerous drug. Nonetheless, it would be many months before I ever smoked again.

SQUARING UP AND STARTING OVER

It was time to pay off my debt. My grandmother gave me $5,000 of the $15,000 I needed. I paid off another $3,500 by selling the Segway. I found a job working with my older brother at a graphic design firm to pay off the remainder. I worked until March and emerged debt-free.

With the burden of debt removed, it was time to go back to school. I had a completely different perspective on life; this was my second chance. I had been sober since October. However, my roommates still smoked marijuana and they all drank. When I first returned to Ohio State, I hated even the smell of marijuana. After a month or so, though, I became curious and wanted to try it again. I was hooked immediately.

Obviously, my parents were going to find out. When they invited me to come home for a family party, I discovered it was an intervention. I told them I knew I had a problem and that I would fix it. I was able to stop using for a month or so but that was all. It didn't seem to affect my medications, and I thought I was okay.

Perhaps I wasn't the best judge of that. I continued to smoke every day for the next couple years. I did, however, completely stay away from alcohol. I enjoyed smoking weed much more, anyway.

NATIONALS

Over the next two years I worked hard to complete my civil engineering degree. During the warmer months, I spent my time practicing waterskiing and coaching other people on the team. It was my greatest passion. I had already won a state championship and now my goal was to win a collegiate waterskiing national championship for Ohio State. Our men's team was very solid, but our women's team needed some work. I spent the entire summer coaching our girls so we'd be ready to compete for a national championship.

Autumn quarter was tournament season. Our team was solid; we won the Great Lakes Conference Tournament and then went on to regionals. At regionals we placed high enough to qualify for nationals for the first time in 29 years. We traveled to the Buda, Texas, near Austin, to compete for the Division II national title. We won it, beating out the University of Texas. We did this without a coach and with very little funding from Ohio State. It had been a long building process and was the proudest accomplishment of my life.

SOME BAD ADVICE

My cousin was only 29 when he passed away unexpectedly. While I was at his funeral in Florida, a relative told me that one of my medications was linked to diabetes. I did a little research on the medication and found it to be true. I continued to take my meds while I was in Florida, but I was hesitant to take them once I returned to Columbus. I had been taking them for more than two years and felt great. My biggest complaint was that they put me to sleep; I couldn't stay out because I would sleep so long the next day. That week there were a few days that I wanted to stay up late. I had a test I needed to cram for and I also wanted to hang out with my friends.

Because of that, I took my medications only once that week. I smoked for the first time in a week because I hadn't had access to weed in Florida. I hung out with my friends, who were happy to see me staying up later than usual. Midweek, I went to see Cleveland rapper Machine Gun Kelly right down the street from my apartment.

I was in my usual state of mind, high as shit. After the show, Machine Gun Kelly came up to the bar to buy some drinks. I passed on the drinks since I'd been sober for more than two years. Instead, I talked to him with other people from the bar. For some reason, I had the feeling the rapper was happy to finally meet me rather than my being happy to meet him. Eventually, I found myself laughing hysterically at nothing. It was the beginning of my second manic episode. Jesus would show up again, signs would reappear, and the worst was yet to come.

When my parents came to see me later in the week, we went to lunch. I ordered an iced tea. When I opened the bottle of tea, I noticed the words, "The Chosen One" on the lid. When my dad picked the lid up, he asked, "Who's the chosen one?" A sign.

The special of the day was fish. I thought fish was something Jesus would eat, and I ordered it. When the waiter said, "You made the right choice!" I knew it was another sign. I should have told my parents that the signs were happening again, but I didn't, and they left town.

It was kind of a wild evening with my friends. When we stopped at a grocery store, one of my friends asked if I wanted to smoke. For once, I hesitated, but I was feeling good, so I took a few hits. The weed intensified the mania. As we bought munchies, I looked at each grocery item as if there were a right answer about what to buy. I looked for signs on the frozen pizza and bags of chips. The psych ward all over again.

At my friend Nick's, we jammed for a while; I laughed my ass off the entire time, while a picture of Jesus looked down on me from above the fireplace. I knew once again that I was the Second Coming. And my friends were in on it.

THE DRIVE AND THE END OF AN ERA

It was 3 A.M., but the night was far from over for me. I hopped into my car, intending to cruise around downtown Columbus and then go home, but the music was blaring and I was singing, and I decided I'd rather head for the highway.

I had no destination in mind. All wanted to do was drive and listen to music. The closest city was Indianapolis, three hours away. The drive was flat and there was nothing to look at but cornfields. I was having the time of my life, though. Everything's great in a manic state.

The music I was listening to seemed written for me and for this particular drive. I could relate the lyrics of every song to something in my life. Some of the songs' lyrics matched up with words on billboards off the side of the interstate. There were also multiple billboards that said things such as "Jesus is Real." This only made me believe more strongly that I was Jesus Christ.

I had no concept of time. I continued to drive and jam out, going faster and faster. On snow-covered road, I accelerated to about 90 miles per hour. All of a sudden my car spun around and went down the highway backwards for about five seconds. I didn't panic. I laughed and spun the car back around. I felt as if someone had protected me. Once again, I was invincible.

Invincible or not, I had a flat tire. I drove to the next exit and tried to find a gas station. The closest one was in the city of Rushville. I'd need quarters to turn on the air compressor, but discovered I'd left my wallet in Columbus.

I went inside and asked the attendant to turn the pump on for me. She told me I'd have to pay. After I went to the restroom to take a piss, I washed my hands, putting them back and forth under the water three times, just as I had during my last manic episode.

When I decided to change my tire, I couldn't find the wrench to loosen the lug nuts. I reached for my cell phone and discovered it, too, was in Columbus. I wanted to call AAA, but I didn't have a card. I should've gone inside and asked to use the gas station phone. Instead, I took my shoes off, stretched my legs across the passenger seat, and lay back with the heat blasting and my music pounding.

I said to myself, "Fuck it!" I drove off, turned west, and decided on the spot to follow the signs west until I got to California. My destination was the mansion in the Hollywood Hills. This mansion was made for Jesus.

Without a wallet or a cell phone and only a quarter-tank of gas, I was on my way. I felt invincible. I flew through the winding back roads and continued to accelerate. The music was pounding, and the flat tire was the last thing on my mind. Although I do not recall red stoplights, the police report said I flew through two of them. I blew past the Rushville police station going 70 mph in a 20 mph zone.

Soon after, I was on the highway and the straightaway gave me a chance to put the pedal to the floor. At 120 miles per hour, I looked in my rearview mirror and saw police lights way back in the distance. I remembered a line from the song "Dynamite" by Taio Cruz, and I opened my sunroof and stuck both hands up in the air with my middle fingers pointed to the police. I thought they'd never catch me. Then everything went black.

SECTION II

-12-
WAKING UP AGAIN

I opened my eyes and saw that I was surrounded by my entire family. I wanted to speak, but there was a breathing tube shoved down my throat. Right away I noticed that I could not move my legs, and there was a fixator drilled into my left arm, a brace around my neck, chest tubes coming out of each side of me, and sensors and IVs all over my body.

I could see in the eyes of my family that this wasn't good. They all looked very sad and concerned. The room was extremely quiet.

Since I couldn't talk I made a motion with the only thing I could move, my right hand. I motioned that I wanted to write something. My hand felt as if it had punched a brick wall, but I was able to write, "Did I hurt anyone?" My family shook their heads. "Am I a cripple?" They shook their heads again. Then I wrote the word "hug" on the pad of paper. My mom gave me a hug. It was the only thing that could comfort me at this time.

I knew I had broken my neck, but what I wanted desperately to know was whether my spinal cord was severed. I had some knowledge of this situation. When my Dad was 32 years old, he was in an automobile accident and injured his spinal cord. Since the cord was only bruised and not severed, he slowly got everything back in about a year's time. I wanted to believe that the same thing was going to happen to me, and I thought about him to keep my mind at ease.

It would be three long days in the ICU before they removed the breathing tube and I could ask questions. Obviously, the first thing I asked was whether my spinal cord was severed. The doctors didn't have the answer quite yet and we would have to wait a few more days for a more thorough assessment. This scared the hell out of me, especially since I couldn't feel somebody touching my legs.

I asked about the accident. I knew I had been going between 120 and 130 miles per hour when I crashed. My family told me I had flipped five times end over end. Wreckage covered a half-mile area. The flips were spaced 25 feet apart at first, and the car finally came to rest upside down in the snow. The paramedics were there right away because the cops had already been on my tail. My dad had a picture of my car from the junkyard on his cell phone. Every inch of the car was destroyed. I couldn't believe I had survived.

Both of my lungs were collapsed, and the chest tubes were helping them heal by removing the nasty fluids and pus in my lungs. I constantly had to cough up secretions, but I was unable to on my own. I needed the help of the nurse who would push down on my stomach so I could cough. I thought I was unable to cough because my lungs were so weak. I later found out that my abdominal muscles were paralyzed. In the many long days to come, I would find out that paralysis affected far more than my legs.

HOPE

I spent five days in the ICU before I was transferred to a regular room. Now I was breathing on my own, but my lungs were recovering slowly. The chest tubes were still in and I would be bedridden for several more weeks. Although I was excited about the day I would get my wheelchair and be able to move around, I enjoyed the company of my friends and family, and the outpouring of support I was receiving.

On my first day in a regular room, five of my friends from school came to visit. My eyes were blood-red like a demon's because the blood vessels in my eyes had burst during the crash. One of my teeth was chipped off, but my friends said they loved to see me smile. I was so happy to see them. They asked me about the crash, to which they said I was a crazy motherfucker. I agreed. I literally was crazy at the time.

I shared my first room with three other patients, and the noise was horrendous. One patient was near death and the nurses were in constantly to check on him. Another kept the TV on all night, so I got no sleep until about 5 A.M. Then rounds, chest x-rays, and blood tests began for the day. The hospital was definitely not a place to rest.

In a few days, the doctors explained that they would be conducting an American Spinal Injury Association (ASIA) test on me. The examination has two parts: sensory and motor. They tested my sensation by using a pin that was dull on one side and sharp on the other. The doctor poked my entire body asked me whether it felt dull, sharp, or if I felt nothing at all. It cary when she poked some areas below my chest I felt nothing.

For the motor portion of the test, the doctor tried to get me to move parts of my body, such as my toes, that were below my injury level, but I couldn't move anything at all.

She then put on a pair of gloves to do a rectal exam, telling me that if she could feel my rectum contract, it meant my spinal cord was still intact. I was so nervous, not about having a finger jammed up my butt, but about what she would find. Surprisingly, I felt very little during the exam, but when she told me that she could feel a rectal contraction, I started to cry, right then and there, with her finger still up in me. I knew I was going to be okay.

The medical staff told me this was very good news. If my spinal cord were severed, I had no chance of getting function back. With my spinal cord still intact, I had a chance of walking again. I once again thought back to what my Dad went through and knew my situation was exactly the same. In a year I'd be back on my feet and slalom skiing again. I was sure the recovery would be tougher than anything I could ever imagine—and it wasn't certain—but at that time there was no doubt in my mind I would walk again. I always had been the luckiest kid in the world, and I refused to believe that my luck wouldn't hold.

The rest of the day, I spent my time trying to fall back to sleep, but the noise in the room made it impossible. I begged the nurses to get me into a new room. It took most of the day, but finally I was transferred.

It wasn't too much better. My roommate had problems with falling. The last time he fell was off a ladder at work, which sent him to the hospital. He was supposed to stay in his bed at all times unless a nurse was there to help him. I asked him where he was from, and he was proud to say he lived right by the Indianapolis Speedway.

I told him that I was in the hospital because I flipped my car five times. At this, he immediately got out of bed and said he wanted to see a kid who was stupid enough to flip his car that many times. He took a good look at me with his evil-looking eyes and managed to get back to his bed

Later on, when he had to walk five feet to the restroom, he got out of bed and fell flat on his face. The next time he had to go to the bathroom, the same thing happened. He didn't want to rely on the nurses and argued with them when he wasn't able to walk on his own. They finally alarmed his bed, but that didn't stop him. At first, it was sort of entertaining to hear him fall and then curse at everyone who tried to help him. After a couple days of this guy, though, I had to get away from him. He brought such negative energy into the room, and I needed to be positive. Once again I pleaded with the nurses for a new room and eventually they brought me to my very own private room. It was like leaving hell and going to heaven.

JUST ME AND JESUS

My own room was quiet, and for once I could think. When my dad came back to Indianapolis after a few days, he brought me my MacBook Air, my iPod, and a few other items. I opened my computer and signed into the wi-fi at Methodist Hospital. The first thing I did was I checked my Facebook, and I was overwhelmed to see how much support I had over the last week or so. There were literally hundreds of people who posted on my wall wishing me the best. Some of the messages read:

> "We all knew you were strong before this but how far you've come in just a week is blowing everyone away, even the doctors! Not only do you heal as fast as Wolverine but your attitude and spirit has been nothing but courageous and comforting to your family. Keep it up, we're all here for you every step of the way! And like I told you, next time I visit I know you'll be kicking ass in rehab. Love you Adam, you're doing beyond amazing!!!!"

> "You're the strongest person I know. The speed of your recovery just amazes me, but if anyone is capable of it, it's you. Love you to pieces, keep it up!"
> :)

I responded:
"OVERWHELMED TO TEARS BY ALL OF THE SUPPORT ON HERE! MY FB BARELY

WORKS!! KEEP THE PRAYERS COMING!
LOVE YOU ALL!"

The support I was receiving made me believe
life would get better. I was ready to do anything and
everything to recover and get back on my feet.

On my first morning in my new room, the
psychiatrist came in to ask how I was doing. He knew I
had bipolar disorder, and he was there to get my
medications in order. He put me on a low dose of
Seroquel—only a fourth of what I had been taking
before the accident. It wasn't enough.

When I was driving my car west to California, I
had once again slipped into the delusion thought that I
was Jesus Christ. After the accident, the signs went
away because there was so much going on that I had no
time to think about them. Once I got my private room,
though, I had all day to think. I also had my laptop, my
iPod, and the television to fuel my thoughts.

My music spoke to me just as it had on the ride
to Indianapolis. The television spoke to me. Once
again, everything was a sign from God. For example,
every song on the new Black- Eyed Peas album referred
to me. I was sinking pretty deeply into the mess I'd
been in before.

That night, the nurse came in with my
medication. Because I thought it wasn't necessary, I
grabbed the pill, pretended to put in my mouth, and
then dropped it on the floor.

Later I called Curtis, my best friend from back
home. I told him to stop what he was doing because he
was about to become part of history. I told him to drive
straight to Indianapolis as fast as he could. He wouldn't

be hurt because I would protect him. I said I was about to have all the money and power in the world, and that I could get him any car he wanted. I told him that my arm and legs would be healed the next day. I needed him to drive across country with me so I could take my place as Jesus in California. I also told him that the book I was writing was the Third Testament of the Bible.

Instead of calling me crazy, he tried to reason with me. He said he would visit me soon. He tried to calm me down because I was talking so fast, and he told me to get some rest.

The next person I called was my brother Aaron. Aaron had visited me nearly every day when I was in the psych ward. He knew what I was like when I talked crazy. I told him I knew the answer to everything. That God spoke to me through music and through television. I said I could predict the future just by listening to music, and that our lives were going to change forever.

He argued with me that I was not Jesus Christ. He reminded me this had happened before and was part of the bipolar disorder. I could not have disagreed more. I had to have him listen to a song so he'd believe me. He was so frustrated he hung up.

Immediately afterward, I fired up my computer and opened chapters of the book I had been writing. I posted four of them on Facebook as a note. In the meantime, my dad had called my mom to tell her that I was saying that I was Jesus Christ again. That sent my mom and aunt rushing to my floor to talk to the nurse.

When the nurse asked me if I had taken my medication, for once I told the truth. She left to get the pill and another med because I was so wired. I fell asleep quickly.

I AM THE SECOND COMING

In the morning, I checked my Facebook to see how many people had commented on my writing. To my surprise, the notes were no longer there. Curtis had called Aaron; together they figured out my password and deleted the notes. They had done me a big favor because the notes talked about how much weed I had smoked and other things I didn't want to share at that point. The signs, however, were growing stronger each day.

The events of the night before made for a hectic morning. Instead of just one psychiatrist, an entire group entered my room. They knew that I hadn't taken my medication. They knew about the phone calls and how I was once again saying that I was Jesus Christ.

Two psychiatrists and three students all dressed in their white medical coats would have intimidated most people. Not me, though, not the Son of God. I knew everything. I had all the answers, and these doctors knew nothing compared to what I knew.

They started to fire questions at me. They wanted to know if I thought I was Jesus Christ. I remembered that when I was in the psych ward, the more I said I was Jesus, the harder it was to get out of there. This time around I lied. I said I had been having those thoughts but they had gone away since I had taken my meds the night before. They asked me why I had not taken them the first time around. I said it was because I wanted to stay up late on my computer and the medication put me to sleep.

The psychiatrists decided to put me on a medication called Risperdal. I would start by taking a two mg. tablet and then eventually move up to four mg. Because the dosage was so small, I felt that they were giving me less medication, which made me think they believed me when I said I no longer thought I was Jesus.

I agreed to take the medications and told them there would be no further problems. Later I found out that the one 300 mg. tablet of Seroquel I was taking was equal to 1 mg of Risperdal, so, in fact, they had put me on a larger dose of a much stronger antipsychotic.

After the doctors left, my mom asked if I still thought I was Christ. I told her a long and rambling story about a sign I had received the day before the accident. The gist of the sign was that she was my mother, but my father was God. I said that Aaron was my twin brother but that we had different fathers, which is why Aaron has brown hair like our father, but I have blond hair and look nothing like my dad.

I explained that it made sense for me to have blond hair and blue eyes because even Hitler knew that the Aryan race was dominant. Hitler received these signs from God that told him about the Second Coming.

My mom was driven to tears. She said I was going to end up in the psych ward again. She asked me if I remembered what that was like and how much hard work I put in to make myself stop thinking that way. The more she made me think about the psych ward, the more sure I was that I was Jesus.

I told my mom that I was being tortured in preparation for being put on the cross. To create world peace, I must first suffer the hardships of being paralyzed. I would suffer for about a year or so. Then on December 21, 2012, which many people thought would be the end of the world, I would be revealed and spread universal peace.

I went on to say that there was already an army of believers who knew of the Second Coming. They were Hollywood celebrities and many of my friends and family. The celebrities were able to read the signs from God and could tell the masses about them through television and other media. I could even look at Facebook and tell which of my friends were the believers.

At this point my mom had heard enough. She walked towards the door crying, but before she left she turned to me and said, "Your dad loves you so much. He raised you since you were a baby and has always been there for you. I can't believe you would think such a thing."

As soon as she left the room, I noticed a soap opera on television. I swear that the first thing one of the characters said was, "Your father and I raised you since you were a baby. We both love you very much."

I thought this was another sign. But this time it made me think that my father actually was my father and that God was trying to tell me this. Still, it would take some convincing and steady medication before the signs disappeared.

-13-
A LONG ROAD AHEAD

I had told my friend Curtis that by morning I would be healed and we would drive across the country to California. But when I woke up, I still couldn't move a thing, not even a toe. Maybe I didn't have the healing powers Jesus was supposed to have. Maybe I was going to heal, but it would take patience and hard work. Patience is a virtue, and God was trying to teach me that lesson. It would take patience to create world peace, and fighting paralysis would be the ultimate teacher of this lesson. These were my training days. When the physical therapists entered my room, they brought along a big lesson about just how far I had to go.

Because the spinal cord regulates blood pressure and my spinal cord was significantly damaged, they wrapped my legs with Ace bandages and tightened an abdominal binder around my waist to elevate my pressure and keep me from blacking out when they sat me up.

Once I was wrapped and ready to go, they pulled me to a sitting position. To my surprise, I had absolutely no sitting balance. They explained to me that my core muscles, not just my legs, also were paralyzed. To sit up I needed the help of two physical therapists holding me on either side. It didn't take long until blackness closed in. The first time I sat up I lasted only about 15 seconds. I was crushed. How was I going to walk again if I could sit up for only 15 seconds?

I had to give it another try. They sat me back up after the darkness cleared. One therapist told me to look straight ahead because it would help keep my blood pressure where it needed to be. My gigantic head was almost too heavy for my weak, recovering neck, but by looking forward I managed to sit up for nearly two minutes. That was the end of physical therapy for the day and my first lesson in patience.

Day by day, stacks of get-well cards and gifts were delivered to my room. The day of my first physical therapy, I had two surprises in the mail. One was an autographed picture of Jim Tressel and a card from him, too. The picture was signed, "The Buckeyes are cheering for you! God Bless! Go Bucks! Jim Tressel."

The card said,
"Dear Adam,
We received word of your recent
car accident. Please know the
Ohio State football family is
cheering for you and wishes you
a complete recovery. May your
faith carry you through the
challenges you are facing. God
Bless!
Sincerely,
Jim Tressel"

It was encouraging to hear that the entire Ohio State football team was behind me. I received this card just before Coach Tressel faced the consequences from the tattoo scandal. I have great respect for this man, and it was very difficult for me to see him resign.

The other gift I received was my favorite. Curtis and his mother presented me with a custom-made blanket covered in pictures of me waterskiing. I cried when I saw it. Waterskiing had been my passion for so long, and I was scared to death I would never do it again. This blanket only pushed me harder to want to get better. My ultimate goal was to return to my life on the water.

The blanket also made for a nice talking point with the cute nurses. They could see who I really was. I was a national champion athlete, and I promised them I would do it again one day. I did not want to be just a paralyzed kid in a bed. This was all just part of a heroic comeback.

Once everyone left for the day, I turned on the TV to watch Fox news. I was seeing signs on television and of all the stations, Fox was speaking most directly to me. That night they had a segment called "Places You Can't Go, But We Did." They showed a video of a very exclusive hotel room in downtown Indianapolis that was created to serve celebrities and other powerful people. The room was lavishly decorated and came with a full staff to cater to a guest's every need. This, I thought, was my next destination. Here I would be treated like a king. There was no reason for me to stay in this gloomy hospital room.

I took out my phone, dialed 0 and asked for the number to Fox News in Indianapolis. I thought the network was reaching out to me. I asked to speak with the highest official in the newsroom at the time. They transferred me to a reporter. I told him I was the Second

Coming of Jesus Christ and that the whole world was about to change—and he would be a part of history. I told him to send just one reporter and camera operator to my room at Methodist Hospital. I didn't want a huge crowd. Instead, the reporter hung up on me. I called another news station and demanded the same thing. Not surprisingly, the response was the same. I became terribly frustrated. When was it going to be my time? I figured I would just have to wait.

THE NEW KING OF AKRON

The next morning, the nurse told me that one of my chest tubes could come out and it would be a painful experience. I had refused to take painkillers because they made me itchy and groggy. I wanted to have a clear head. To my surprise, when the chest tube was pulled, I felt nothing. This event showed me I could no longer feel pain from the chest down—and that was some superhero shit. Maybe Jesus was the same way when he was nailed to the cross.

Soon after, it was time for my bed bath. One nurse looked around the room at all the cards, flowers, and gifts I had received. "Look at the king!" she said. "Now we need to make him look like a king!" I laughed and thought to myself that they were in on my secret. They were both believers, and they knew I was the Second Coming.

They took off my hospital gown to give me my bath. By this point I no longer cared who saw me naked. One nurse started with my legs. I asked her if she could please use warm water. "Honey, this is warm water," she said. I couldn't believe it. Not only could I not feel pain, but I also couldn't feel hot or cold. It

99

seemed like every day I would discover more and more things that were wrong with me.

Later the physical therapists went to work wrapping my legs and fastening the abdominal binder around my waist. My goal was to beat the two-minute mark I set the day before. This time I was able to sit for eight minutes before the world faded to black.

THE ANGELS AND THE OTHERS

As I lay back down and regained clarity in my vision, my mind raced. I decided the nurses were angels. There had to be more angels taking care of me. There was a bald-headed guy I was sure was an angel and a girl who was a nonbeliever. I thought God was going to bring the angels and nonbelievers together so they could witness the miracle of Jesus Christ. I sat up again, and this time I lasted 12 minutes. I was making progress, but I was a long way from being able to sit up all day.

It was the weekend of Winter Conference for the Midwest Collegiate Water Skiers, that year at Purdue, about an hour away from Indianapolis.

My friends from the Cincinnati Waterski Team arrived that afternoon. They brought me a wooden cutout of the state of Ohio my friend Steve had cut out in wood shop. On it were the words "Team Ohio" and a picture of all of the Ohio teams from the Midwest regionals the year before. The entire team had signed the back.

While they were there, I analyzed each of them and tried to classify them as angels or nonbelievers. I believed that they were all angels except for one of the girls. This classification system was rapidly becoming an obsession.

Later that evening, friends from the Ohio State Waterski Team stopped by on their way to Purdue. Once again, I picked out which of my friends were angels and which were not. I think my mood was surprising to them. I was cracking jokes and laughing hysterically. I continued to think that the paralysis was only temporary and all part of a master plan. The angels knew this and that I would be okay. The ones that were very concerned were the nonbelievers. Three of my friends I thought were not angels because they seemed to be the most concerned about me.

After they left, I checked my Facebook page. As I looked through my friends list, I carried out the angel/nonbeliever sorting process again. I thought that Facebook was a tool created to spread the word about the Second Coming.

That evening I watched the Cleveland Cavaliers game on my laptop. The Cavs, who were on a 26-game losing streak, were playing the Philadelphia 76ers. The game went into overtime and the Cavs won without LeBron James, who had left to join the Miami Heat. My Facebook post said, "I told y'all we don't need LeBron." I thought that as long as I was watching the game, I could decide the fate of it. The Cavs won that night because I wanted them to.

LeBron James was born in Akron, Ohio, and claimed to be the King of Akron. I thought that as Jesus Christ I was not only the new king of the world, but also the new king of Akron. People used to worship LeBron in Northeast Ohio. He was the hometown hero.

But now it was time for a new king to take over. That king was I.

THE ANTICHRIST

Another morning, another chest x-ray, and another visit from the psychiatrists. Once again they asked me about the signs and if I believed that I was Jesus Christ. Once again I lied, but by the way they were talking to me I should've known they were on to me. Every morning my mom waited in the hall to talk to them after I finished telling my lies. She would tell them about the signs and about how strongly I felt that I was Jesus. As one doctor said, "We know he's trying to keep this from us. We deal with these situations all the time." My dosage of my medication was larger each night.

Later, the physical therapists came through my door in their green scrubs. This time the baldheaded angel from the day before was accompanied by the dark-haired nonbeliever woman and another man. This man talked like Cheech Marin. He joked around and pretended this was his first day on the job.

It was time to beat the 12-minute mark I had set the day before. As they wrapped my legs and put on the abdominal binder, Cheech kept me laughing. This time around I lasted 27 minutes, more than twice as long as the day before. They laid me back down until I was ready for round two. This time around I sat up for 35 minutes.

Cheech congratulated me, and when the therapists left it occurred to me that maybe hippies like the original Cheech knew the secret of the Second Coming. Part of the way to spread world peace was to get everyone off alcohol and on marijuana. Alcohol was created by man, and marijuana was created by God. Whom should we trust? Alcoholics can become mean and violent, while stoners are usually laid back and happy. I thought that as Jesus I would show the world it was wrong to make marijuana illegal. That illegality was part of a widespread conspiracy.

The marijuana plant has an array of beneficial uses. The earliest known woven fabric was apparently of hemp, and over the centuries the plant was used for food, incense, cloth, rope, and much more.

Hemp seed oil can be used in biodiesel engines. This use scared the oil companies because it would be much cheaper than their products.

Marijuana also has many medicinal purposes. It's obvious that it gives smokers the munchies. For people who have no appetite, marijuana would be a great medicine. It can also control nausea and vomiting associated with chemotherapy. It can decrease intraocular pressure and help with neurological and movement disorders.

Most interesting are its uses in curing cancer. A Harvard study released on April 17, 2007, shows that the active ingredient in marijuana, THC, cuts tumor growth in common lung cancer in half and significantly reduces the ability of the cancer to spread. If marijuana were to become legal, pharmaceutical companies would lose billions on a drug that could be grown for free.

I was sure there was a giant government conspiracy behind marijuana's being illegal. It was my job to spread the word about weed and to make it accepted around the entire world. It was going to be me

versus the President of the United States: Barack
Obama, the antichrist.

Positive

The only good thing about this manic episode
was that it kept my mind off worrying about my
condition. Not once did I think about the fact that I
might be paralyzed for the rest of my life. In a year I
would be up and walking, waterskiing, and doing
everything I did before my accident. I would come out
as the leader of the new world.

Music and media continued to speak to me all
the time. I had truly lost my mind, and I looked for a
meaning in everything. As my mind raced, I thought it
was appropriate for me to be from Stow, Ohio. It made
sense that Jesus would be stowed away in a place called
Stow. It also made sense that I was from Ohio, which
was nicknamed the "Heart of It All." As I watched an
Ohio State basketball game, I realized that the Block O
in the stands looked like a halo.

One evening, I tried to make believers out of
some of the nurses. I had the first nurse sit down and
talk to me. I told her that I was the Second Coming of
Jesus Christ and could answer any question she had. Of
course she thought I was crazy, but she listened for a
short while. I told her it was not fair that the nurses did
all the work but the doctors got all the money. In the
future, I said, money wouldn't matter. The world was
going to live in complete harmony, and we were going
to share everything we owned.

The next nurse who came in was much more
laid back. I shared my thoughts about the relative merits
of alcohol and marijuana. She agreed and said she
definitely liked to smoke every once in a while.

Because she was a smoker, I thought that she was an angel and that there was no need to convince her that I was Jesus. The first nurse, on the other hand, was against weed and was one of the nonbelievers.

This episode went in the nurses' report, which the psychiatrists would hear about the next day. Finally the doctors had documented proof that I was claiming to be Jesus Christ. Not only was it reported by the first nurse, but also by the one I thought was an angel. The doctors questioned me about the previous night, and I had to admit I still thought I was the Second Coming. They told me they were going to up my medication to the maximum dose. It would take time, they said, but the signs eventually would go away. I was to keep them informed and be totally honest about what I was thinking and how I was feeling. They could not help me unless I was willing to tell the truth.

THE ANOINTING OF THE SICK

The previous day I had requested to speak with the Catholic chaplain, and that morning he came to see me. He was an African American man dressed in a cassock. He had just returned from Africa, where he had traveled to spread Catholicism.

I told him that I was constantly seeing signs and it seemed like God was speaking to me. I asked him if there could be some explanation for this. He said that in times of need, God will reach out to people in mysterious ways. Since I was in such a time, he asked if I was interested in the anointing of the sick. This ritual is administered to bring spiritual and even physical strength during an illness. He took out oil and made the sign of the cross on my forehead and said, "Through this holy anointing may the Lord in his love and mercy help you with the grace of the Holy Spirit." Then he placed oil on my hands and prayed, "May the Lord who frees you from sin save you and raise you up."

I held his hand as he said a prayer for me. After the prayer, he went to lead Mass and said he would dedicate the Mass to me. I told my mom it was important for her to be at Mass and I waited for it to be broadcast on the hospital station.

As I watched the Mass, I saw my mother walk into the room and take a seat. The priest said he was dedicating this Mass to a young man named Adam and asked that everyone pray for my recovery. During the Mass, he talked about the story of Adam and Eve. This was the beginning of my study of the Bible. Over the next couple of years, I would learn much more about it.

After Mass, my other chest tube was removed. This milestone meant I could be transferred to another hospital to begin the rehab process.

A DISAGREEMENT AND A CHOICE

My family already had been researching which hospitals were the best for spinal cord injuries. Our first choice was Cleveland Metro, which is the number two spinal cord injury rehab hospital in the country. The second choice was Edwin Shaw of Akron General because it was closest to home. The final choice was The Ohio State University Medical Center. We told the discharge social worker about these choices; he said he would find out which hospitals had availabilities.

He came back later and explained that Edwin Shaw was the only hospital that had an opening. My mom said she wanted to wait for an opening at

Cleveland Metro. The social worker told us it might take several days for that to happen. All *I* wanted was to get the hell out of Indianapolis. My mom argued that I should wait for Cleveland Metro because I would receive the best rehab possible and that a few more days in Indianapolis wouldn't be that bad. The social worker said it was my decision, so I told him to look into Edwin Shaw.

I thought it didn't matter which hospital I went do. No matter what, I was going to heal, and I was going to be walking. Edwin Shaw was closest to home and closest to my friends and family. I didn't want to wait around to go to Cleveland. I wasn't as familiar with Cleveland as I was with Akron and Columbus. I wanted to go to Edwin Shaw and eventually transfer to Ohio State to be close to my friends.

My mom started to cry. She begged me to wait to go to Cleveland Metro. She left the room in frustration, and while she was gone, she called a family friend who knew of a boy who went to Cleveland Metro because of a football accident. He was walking again. The friend got in contact with the boy's mom and had her call Cleveland Metro to explain the situation. Later that day, my mom received a call from the spinal cord specialist at Cleveland Metro. Their only concern was that they thought that I would not be able to do three hours of rehab a day with a fixator in my arm. However, they called back later to say they would accept me into the program.

My mom rushed into the room to share the good news. She smiled from ear to ear as she told me about the opening at Cleveland Metro. I told her that I still wanted to be close to home and that I wanted to go to

Edwin Shaw. My mom went into action. She called my dad, my brother, and several other people and asked them to try to convince me to go to Cleveland Metro.

My dad was the first to call. He was angry and he talked to me like I was an idiot for choosing Edwin Shaw. I hung up on him. He called me right back, but I didn't answer. Next to call was my older brother, and I blew him off, too. Then my friend, Ben, called me. Ben was one who had visited me with the waterski team and was one of those I thought was an angel. He told me that once I got to Edwin Shaw, I would be stuck there. There was no way that insurance was going to allow me to transfer to Ohio State. He said Cleveland Metro was the shit and that there was no reason to go anywhere else.

I would not take advice from my mom. I would not take advice from my dad or my brother. But I did take the advice of a friend I thought was an angel. We left for Cleveland the next morning.

-14-
AT HOME IN CLEVELAND

When the paramedics pulled me out of the ambulance at Cleveland Metro, I asked if I could stay outside for a few minutes. It wasn't the cleanest air in the world, but it sure felt good to breathe it in. As they wheeled me into the hospital, I saw a man with a Cleveland Indians hat and another with a Cincinnati Reds hat. I thought that the 'C' on each of these hats stood for Christ. These people would protect me. I was assigned to room 705 on the seventh floor. All I could think of was seventh heaven.

I was on the spinal cord injury floor. I asked my new roommate if he minded telling me how he was injured. He told me that he was shot in the back and that the bullet hit his spine. He was trespassing on someone else's property, and an Arab man shot him in the back without warning.

For some reason, I didn't believe him. I thought it was all an act. In fact, I thought that the whole hospital was one big act. The patients weren't actually injured. They were only pretending to be. I was the only one there with a real spinal cord injury. The doctors and nurses had been carefully chosen to take care of me and to be part of the act. They had been rehearsing for years, and now that I was there, the show had finally started.

I knew it wasn't the time for them to acknowledge me as Christ. This was my time to train for the time I would become the leader of the New World. But when would that day come?

Perhaps on a holiday. Valentine's Day was coming up, but I thought that was too soon. The next holiday was Easter. That made perfect sense. On Easter, Jesus rose from the dead. On that same day, some 2,000 years later, I would walk out of the hospital. This gave me two-and- a-half months to learn to walk again, even though I couldn't move my lower body at all.

The first evening of my stay at Cleveland Metro, I looked over at the television movie my roommate was watching. It was *Resident Evil: Apocalypse*. In this movie the main character, Alice, is exposed to a virus that gives her superhuman strength, speed, and agility. She has to work with a team to fight off a zombie apocalypse. During the movie, she keeps looking into a book that tells her what to do next. I thought she was reading the signs from God—that Alice represented me and what my role would be in the future. It scared me to think that in 2012 there was going to be a zombie apocalypse and I was supposed to save the world from it. I thought that my roommate had purposely played this movie to warn me of the future.

After the movie, the nurse came in to administer my suppository. Not only could I not take a piss, but I also could not poop on my own. She placed a few Chux pads underneath me because I went to the bathroom in the middle of the night. The nurse said she would come and clean me up when that happened. I also had to be turned every four hours so I wouldn't develop any bedsores. The whole thing was upsetting. Not only could I not sleep through the night, but I also had to wake up in my own shit.

After not much sleep, I was wakened at 7 A.M. to get ready for a long day of therapy.

THERAPY TIME

It was a little like Indianapolis. My legs were wrapped and the binder placed around my waist. This time, though, I got dressed. The nurse pulled a pair of track pants out of my drawer and rolled me from side to side as she pulled them up. She helped me put my shirt on and finally strapped on my size 13½ Velcro shoes.

To get me out of bed, they brought in a Hoyer lift, which is basically a crane for people. They lifted me up in the air and dropped me into the chair. When I sat down, my head fell back because the headrest wasn't positioned properly. It hurt to hold my head up. That was only the first problem I ran into.

From sitting up so fast, I started to pass out and yelled for the nurse. She told me to relax as she tilted the wheelchair back. My vision slowly came back into focus.

After my head cleared, I was wheeled to the occupational therapy room. I had never heard of occupational therapy, so I had no idea what I was getting myself into.

Whatever it was, the occupational therapist I had was great. First she did an evaluation to measure my grip strength, pinch strength, and dexterity. She also measured the strength of my wrist and my arm, and the angles to which I could bend them and my fingers.

After the evaluation, she began my therapy, giving me something called theraputty and telling me to squeeze it with my right hand. She showed me several exercises to do to strengthen my hand. Next she gave me an assortment of plastic clothespins with different tensions. To strengthen my pinch, I had to squeeze the clothespins open and put them on a rod. Each color was a different strength, but I was not able to make it through all the colors. When I was waterskiing my grip was very strong. That was all gone, and I would have to work to regain it.

After occupational therapy, I was directed to speech therapy. I was unaware that there are blood vessels that go down your spine and are connected to your brain. If any of those were damaged during the accident, I could have problems with my brain. The speech therapist started off by giving me a few numbers and asking me to repeat them back to her. She then went on to give me four numbers, than five, then six, and so on. She got all the way up to nine numbers.

She then told me we were going to do the same thing but backwards. She would say 423 and I would have to say 324. Once again, we went to nine numbers, and I never missed a single one. She was very impressed. I was happy to know that I was all still there mentally.

Next she said several words and asked me to repeat them. She added a word each time, and I had no problems with the task.

The final challenge, though, was very difficult. She read me a paragraph and asked me to repeat it to her. I barely remembered anything that she had said. My perfect day had dipped to mediocre.

After lunch, it was on to physical therapy. I was curious to see how physical this therapy could be in my condition. All I could do was move my right arm and hand. My legs were paralyzed, and my left arm was in a fixator. The physical therapist used a wooden slide board to transfer me from my chair to an elevated mat. Once I was on the mat, she told me we would start with stretches. I was surprised by how stiff my legs were. I shouldn't have been. After all, they hadn't moved for four weeks.

After stretching me out for a good half-hour, she brought over an eight-pound dumbbell for me to work my right arm. She started to instruct me but I stopped her and told her that I used to lift a great deal. I said I would do supersets of chest press, biceps curls, triceps extensions, and lateral raises. Before I was injured, I was doing chest presses with 90-pound dumbbells, and I bench pressed nearly 300 pounds. Now I was doing a tenth of that. I had a long way to go to get my strength back.

THIS IS ALL TOO REAL

The nightly routine always the same: bed bath, followed by a bowel treatment, followed by my fourth round of medications for the day. I stared at pictures of my family my mom had hung up around the room. They inspired me to return to the person I was before the accident. It was going to take a while to adjust to not being able to sleep through the night. I wasn't able to dream because I was always being awakened during REM sleep—and I wanted to live through my dreams. I wanted to be running and waterskiing again. I even had a dream catcher above my bed in hopes it would help.

Getting my vitals checked every night seemed like overkill. Shitting the bed every night was not something I got used to. I lay there helpless while some stranger cleaned me up. Once that was done and the smell was gone, it was time to get those last few precious hours of sleep. Many times, though, I was not able to fall back to sleep. Tired and groggy, I would have to push through several hours of therapy.

During the stretching part of my physical therapy, I noticed that I couldn't feel the pain of the stretch, unlike the man lying next to me, who screamed in pain. I took this chance to help him out. I told him that pain could be controlled not only by medication but also by the mind. I told him to try not to think so much about the pain he was going through. He calmed down a little bit, but he was still feeling it.

Soon I had measurements taken for my power chair. I couldn't wait for it to arrive because it would give me freedom to move around on my own. Before I received it, I had to be pushed to go anywhere, and since the nurses didn't have the time to be pushing me around all day, I was often left in one place for long periods of time.

I spent a great deal of time analyzing the patients around me. I still thought the whole scene was an act—that the patients, doctors, nurses, and therapists were all in on this together, but, wow, was it good acting! Some were missing limbs, which is pretty hard to fake. Seeing the patients made me start to question my perceptions, and I slowly slipped back into reality. Nonetheless, the idea that I was the Second Coming stayed with me for quite a while.

GAINING INDEPENDENCE AND HOPE

While I was in my manic state, I didn't just

114

believe I might walk again. I *knew* I would walk again.
I was the most positive, upbeat person on the spinal
cord injury floor.

Slowly I gained back some of my independence.
I started off in a situation where my wheelchair had to
be pushed everywhere. Eventually, though, I had my
own power wheelchair to get myself around.
Nonetheless, I had limits. I had to stay on hospital
property, so for the next few months it would be my
prison. I made the best of it. There was a great deal of
the world left to explore. Once I got my wheelchair, no
one ever found me on the spinal cord injury floor
except during therapy. We had to sign out every time
we left the floor, but because I left so often they
eventually just let me go without having to sign out.

I loved to go to the room that overlooked
downtown Cleveland. I would dream about being the
king of the city as well as the rest of the world. My
favorite thing to do was to listen to my iPod and
explore the hospital. At this point, my music was still
talking to me but it was not as meaningful as it was
back in Indianapolis. I would go down to the main floor
and fly up and down the hallways. My wheelchair was
very fast and fun to drive around. On the main floor, I
found a room with a bunch of large pillars lined up. I
would swerve around the pillars in my power chair,
which reminded me of skiing through a slalom course.
When my brother came to see me, I'd have him time
me to see how quickly I could get around the course.
This became my favorite game.

As I wandered around the hospital, I was no
doubt the friendliest patient they had ever seen. I made
friends with everyone—the custodians, the cafeteria

workers, the lady directing traffic into the hospital, and many of the patients. Everyone knew who I was, and I thought the entire staff knew of the Second Coming of Jesus Christ. I would smile and say hello to anyone wearing a cross or a hat with a "C" on it. I thought that to them, meeting me was probably like meeting a celebrity.

I eagerly awaited the day that at least one of these people would verbally affirm to me that I was Jesus, but I figured they would wait until my training was over. First I needed to learn how to walk again. Then I would have to learn everything about religion and all about the problems I would have to fix in this world. I continued to look forward to walking on Easter, so I worked as hard as I could in therapy to ensure that my miracle would come.

So far, there were no signs that my legs were coming back. My dad said his legs improved after a few weeks, and I had been in Cleveland for almost two months. Every night before I went to sleep, I would try to move anything, but nothing ever happened. It became so discouraging that I quit trying. Then one night after I got my bed bath, the nurse asked me to try and move my toes. I was hesitant even to try because I knew they wouldn't budge. But when I looked down, I saw them moving. The nurse laughed and I cried. It was a sign that everything was going to be okay. It gave me newfound hope that I was going to walk again.

I had the nurse hand me my cell phone, and the first person I called was my mom. She was just arriving home from the hour-long drive to the hospital. I told her the news, and she was beyond excited. She said she had just been thinking how great it would be if I were to call her and tell her that I had moved something. Sure enough, her dream had come true. She went inside to tell my dad and the rest of the family who were at my house. They all started to cry when they heard the news. My dad went out and bought three cases of beer to celebrate. Their prayers had been answered.

I went through my phone list and called more family members and a bunch of my close friends. They were all so excited, and I brought many of them to tears. I then posted on Facebook that I moved my toes, and I got more likes than I'd ever seen before. I was now completely convinced that I would walk out of there on Easter. Once again, I tried to move something every night before I went to bed. So far, only my toes would move. It was discouraging, but I just thought it was going to take a little longer than I had expected. It would happen, though, because God was on my side.

ADDITIONAL THERAPY

The next morning, I woke up to the daily visit from my doctor. I told him the news from the night before. I asked him if this was a sign that everything was going to come back. He didn't
seem too excited about the news. He told me that any return is good, but he could not say anything to affirm that everything was coming back. In spite of his attitude, I was convinced that it only was a matter of time before I was back on my feet. I pushed myself harder in therapy than I ever had before.

At Cleveland Metro, I did therapy five days a week for three-and-a-half hours a day. But I felt this wasn't enough. Now that I had my power wheelchair, I could take part in other activities that were offered through the hospital. I wanted to take advantage of everything. So I attended art therapy and music therapy. I felt that the more I would do, the quicker I would heal. I tried to attend every session of every type of therapy.

In art therapy, we would do various projects, making everything from clay bowls to jewelry. I enjoyed doing art, even though it was frustrating having just one hand to work with. I really believed in music therapy. The music therapist explained that there are studies showing that music helps people heal. So I took part in drum circles and jammed out with various instruments to all different kinds of music. I listened to my iPod constantly because the therapist said it would help. I focused on tapping my feet to the beat even though I could not move anything yet. I was told that this would make some sort of connection to my brain.

Taking part in these activities made the time pass quickly. There weren't too many people in the hospital who took part in these activities, so the various therapists were excited to have someone like me show up on a regular basis. We also played on the Wii as part of recreational therapy. Eventually, though, I didn't play as much because I got tired of the two 15-year-old kids with spinal cord injuries who destroyed me at every game.

FRIENDS

Since most of the patients on the floor were much older than I, I hung out with two 15-year-olds the most. One of them had suffered a broken back and spinal cord injury doing what he loved most: motocross. He was left a paraplegic, but still had the use of both hands. The other teen was doing something

118

much less dangerous. He was hanging upside down on a pull-up bar at a friend's house when the bar broke loose. He came crashing down on his head, breaking his neck at C7. He was left a quadriplegic without the use of either of his hands. It was disheartening to see two kids who were so young having to experience something this tragic.

The boy who was in the motocross accident was discharged rather quickly because he could use his hands, and after about five weeks there wasn't too much more to be done for him. The other boy and I had to work hard in occupational therapy to try to regain the use of our hands. This kept us in therapy much longer than Motocross Boy. I spent much more time with the boy who broke his neck, so I became much closer to him. He also had two sisters who were closer to my age; they stayed with him and took care of him. I became very good friends with them as well.

I wanted to help this boy keep his spirits up, and I think my positive attitude and outlook really did help him. I told them my story about how I thought I was Jesus, so they started to call me Jesus. I constantly received cookies and candy, so I often left them in his room. I certainly had more than enough to share. I tried to remind him that we both were going to walk again, but I do not think he believed it as much as I did. When I moved my toes, he became discouraged because he hadn't moved anything yet. I reminded him that I had been injured longer and that it was just a matter of time before he moved something.

Eventually he joined me in wandering the hospital and racing me up and down the hallways. I tried to get him to go outside with me, but for a while it was too cold for him. His body had a hard time regulating temperature, and he would shake profusely when it was even chilly. However, I was outside as soon as the air warmed up only slightly. I loved the fresh air and roaming around outside the hospital while listening to music. Once the temperature went up consistently, I invited my younger friend to go outside again. However, when he did it, he became very upset; it reminded him too much of playing sports. Because I was focusing on making other people happy, I was able to keep my mind off my own situation, at least most of the time.

THE ELBOW

In the accident, I had severely dislocated my left elbow, which required that I have a nasty-looking metal external fixator drilled into the bones in my left arm; four screws held my elbow at a 90-degree angle for six weeks. A year earlier, I was with the waterski team in Florida and saw my friend Ben take a serious fall that dislocated his elbow. He had to keep his arm in a sling for six weeks and then do months of therapy to get the arm to straighten out. He was told it would never be straight again, but he recovered full motion, and the injury doesn't affect him in any way. After talking to Ben, I wasn't worried. I knew that my arm was going to heal just like his.

After six weeks, I was put under with anesthesia, and when I woke up the fixator was gone. Just seeing my arm without a giant metal contraption on it was a relief. The orthopedist told me that when he removed the fixator, he ranged my arm to see how far it would straighten out. He said that it wouldn't go much past 90 degrees. That was scary. Would I really have the use of only my right arm for the rest of my life? But that's what Ben had heard, too, and he defied the odds. So would I.

When I saw my occupational therapist the next day, she said that the therapy would help me straighten out my arm. However, I had very little movement in my left hand. I thought that the lack of motion was caused by being locked up in the fixator. I was wrong. The therapist said that the reason my left hand wasn't moving was because of the spinal cord injury. My hand was paralyzed, and I could only move a few fingers at the knuckle.

I burst into tears. Not only did I have to worry about not being able to straighten my arm, but I also might be without my left hand for the rest of my life. The therapist stepped in, though, and told me that therapy might be able to fix both of the problems.

We first started working on my elbow. It was very stiff after being held in place for six weeks. It hurt like hell as we slowly straightened it out. The therapist would pull on my arm and hold it to a point that was bearable for me until I couldn't take it any longer. Then we would repeat the process.

When I was not at therapy, my homework was to push down on my arm and straighten it as much as I could throughout the day and night. Every day we would measure the angle of my arm to see what progress we had made—and every day we *did* see progress, which was a huge relief. I did more and more to work my arm. My therapist would strap weights around my wrist and I would hang my arm over the side of the wheelchair until I couldn't take the pain.

After several weeks, my arm was only 15 degrees shy of being completely straight. But then I hit a plateau, and no matter how much therapy I did, the arm would not become any straighter. Considering what the doctor had told me, I was very happy with the progress I'd made.

My left hand still had all sorts of problems. My pinky finger was always stuck straight out and was numb to the point where I could barely feel it. My index finger originally had shooting pains go through it all day; later the pain stopped and my finger only itched. I would take an itchy finger over shooting pains any day. This finger also tended to curl up. Originally I had no movement in it, but one day it started to move at the knuckle. Now I had some movement in all of my fingers, which I thought was a sign that my hand was coming back.

Once I got that slight movement back in my index finger, I was able to make a very weak pinch between my thumb and my index finger, which allowed me to start therapy on my left hand. We did tasks that should have been very simple; they proved to be quite difficult instead. It took me forever just to pick up tiny pegs out of a piece of wood. These tasks really tested my patience. The therapist had me squeeze the theraputty, but I couldn't even make a dent in it. She measured my grip, and every time it came out to zero pounds.

After weeks of not seeing any progress, I doubted that my hand would ever come back. I thought of all the things I might never do again. My main concern was whether I would waterski again. Was that over now? I was still convinced I would walk again, but having the use of only one hand would put a limit to what I could do. This realization was a huge reality check. It *finally* occurred to me that maybe I was *not* the Second Coming of Jesus Christ. Once again, it dawned on me that perhaps Jesus was just reaching out to help me. Maybe the signs meant that He was there for me and not that I was He. Apparently I did not have magical healing powers. But I was still young, and time would forever be on my side.

GETTING OUT OF PRISON

For the three months I was in the hospital, patients were allowed to leave on only two occasions. The first was a day pass that permitted us to leave the hospital for the day and return the same night. The second was an overnight pass: we could leave for the day, stay overnight at home, and return following morning. Every morning I saw these two dates on the dry-erase board in my room, and I would count down the days until I could go back out into the world.

I was in the hospital for about two-and-a-half months before my day pass came. I decided to meet up with friends and family at the nearby South Park Mall. This was the first time I had been driven anywhere since the trip in the ambulance from Indianapolis to Cleveland, when I couldn't see anything. This time I could see the road ahead of me. I felt comfortable until we got onto the highway. The van accelerated to get up to speed, and it reminded me of when I took off through those back roads in Indiana. I was nervous and on edge throughout the entire trip and was relieved when we made it to where my friends and family were waiting.

I couldn't believe how excited I was to be

somewhere as commonplace as a mall. Being in the hospital for three months really made me appreciate the outside world. It must be a feeling similar to what people get when they get out of prison. I thought about what my life would have been like if I'd killed someone in the accident and been sentenced to prison. I knew that when I left the hospital, I would never again take anything for granted.

Being in public was a new experience. I noticed that people stared at me and treated me differently. Kids in particular could not take their eyes off me. Maybe they were just jealous that I got to ride around in what looked like a toy. When their parents saw that the kids were staring, they would try to move them along. I also never heard the words "excuse me" more in my life. Parents pushed their kids out of my way, and people constantly said they were sorry when they were just slightly ahead of me in my path. I even had a man stop me and say he'd pray for me to walk again. I wanted to be treated the way I was before the accident, but I was quickly realizing I might have to become accustomed to a new lifestyle.

-15-
HOME AGAIN FOR GOOD?

After three-and-a-half months in the hospital, it was finally time to return home. However, a long list of modifications had to be made to our house before my occupational therapist would deem it suitable for me. If it was not ready, I would have to go to a nursing home.

My dad and my uncle Vince worked hard for more than a month to get the house ready for me. Because there were steps going into every entrance, my dad had to buy a lift to get me into the house. He could have built a ramp, but it would have been an eyesore to make it ADA-compliant. We were thrilled when members of my engineering honorary contacted my family to say they were willing to come up from Columbus and build a ramp for free. Ultimately, though, we decided to put the lift in the garage.

To install the lift, my Dad and uncle created a new doorway going from the garage into our TV room. This was the biggest project, but many more changes were required to ready the house for me. They had to widen multiple doorways so my wheelchair could fit and I could navigate. The one thing they didn't have finished was a handicap-accessible bathroom. Although it wasn't required for me to come home, it sure would've been nice to have.

About a month after I got home, my uncle came

up from Florida and worked with my dad to strip the upstairs bathroom and get it ready for me. Our neighbor was in construction and wanted to help, so he donated a roll-in shower and a handicap-accessible sink. It was amazing how generous people were!

Until the bathroom was finished, my mom had to give me a bed bath every morning. I also used a suppository every night as I did in the hospital. I woke up every morning in my own feces, and my mom had to clean it up. Once the bathroom was finished, it was such a relief to be able to take a shower and go to the bathroom over a toilet. Strangely, however, a shower began to feel more like a chore than a pleasure. Because I no longer could feel hot and cold from the chest down, a shower no longer was as enjoyable as it had been before the accident.

MY NEW TOY

I had been using a loaner chair from the hospital as I waited for the permanent chair to be delivered to my house. The chair was a top-of-the-line Permobil; it was lime green and stood out wherever I went. It had headlights, tail lights, and even blinkers and hazards. It tilted back and reclined. The foot rests adjusted at the push of a button, and it rose up and down, which was nice because I could sit at high-top tables at restaurants or reach something up high. The company billed my insurance an outrageous $48,000 for the chair.

My dad was self-employed, so he had no benefits. My mom got a job in food service at a local high school, which came with great insurance. Without it, my family would have been bankrupt. Just the week I spent in the ICU cost $250,000. Insurance covered medical supplies, therapy, and everything we needed.

DEPRESSION

A depression that started a few weeks before I left the hospital continued and worsened once I got home. I thought I should have been walking by Easter or at least have been able to do more than just wiggle my toes. I became angry with God and angry at the world. I could *not* imagine being in a wheelchair for the rest of my life, but it looked as if that might be the case. I was losing hope, and I took most of it out on my mom.

Every morning when she came to get me up, I had a tantrum. I screamed and shook the bed and threw whatever I could reach. I would yell out things such as, "Why did this happen to me? Why, God?" My mom always stayed strong and allowed me to get it all out. She never once cried or yelled at me. Sometimes she would leave the room until I stopped screaming and hollering. She always reassured me that life would get better, but every day I lost hope again.

One morning I became so angry with God that I looked over at the crucifix on my wall, flicked it off, and yelled, "Fuck you!" My mom told me to take it back and that I should thank God for saving me from a crash that could have killed me. I had been given a second chance at life and I should be thankful. I immediately regretted what I did and prayed for forgiveness. I needed God on my side and this was not the way to win Him over.

ADAM AND AARON

Eventually, my mom had to go back to work

and my brother Aaron took care of me. He had recently graduated from the University of Akron in nursing, so this arrangement worked out perfectly. I didn't scream and yell at my brother every morning; I kept my emotions to myself. Instead, every morning we would check to see if I had any more movement in my legs. We did not see any progress, which, over time, became very discouraging. One morning, however, I saw that I was able to move my right leg in and out. This gave me a small glimmer of hope that things were coming back. It wasn't enough, though, to lift me out of my funk.

I wore a Foley catheter the entire time in the hospital and for the first month after I got out. This catheter stayed in all the time and connected to a drainage bag attached to my leg. One day, I saw nothing in the drainage bag. Suddenly, I felt something I hadn't felt since the night of my accident. I had to pee. I was so excited to have this feeling. My mom and brother thought my catheter was clogged, so we took it out.

As soon as we removed, I started to piss all over the place. I would push and the stream would get stronger. I thought I had regained control of my bladder. I sat there laughing as I peed all over myself. I was so happy to do something as simple as go to the bathroom. My mom and Aaron laughed and told me to stop, but I couldn't. When it finally did stop, we got a straight catheter to see if there was any more left. After cathing, I put out 1600 mL of urine. My bladder was overflowing, as it usually could hold only between 300 mL and 400 mL.

I called my spinal cord doctor and explained the situation to him. I was so excited that I could go to the

ADAM HELBLING

bathroom again without the help of a catheter.
However, he explained that my bladder was just
overflowing, which was why I was able to pee. This
news was extremely discouraging. He recommended
that I stop using a Foley catheter and switch to a
straight catheter. This was something I would have to
do every four hours. I was not looking forward to it, but
I took his advice. At least I no longer had a bag of urine
hanging from my leg.

I had frequent accidents that required many
changes of clothes. This new procedure also meant that
my mom had to wake me up halfway through the night
to help me cath. I had a good number of accidents,
which was very unpleasant to wake up to. I could not
feel pain below my level of injury but I could feel some
pain when I cathed. Eventually, though, the pain went
away.

I got tired of wetting the bed. Then one of the
nurses told me about condom catheters. This was like a
condom, but the tip connected to a drainage bag. Using
them allowed me to sleep through the night.
Occasionally it would come off and I would have
accidents, but they were much less frequent than before.

SEARCHING FOR HOPE

As I became more and more discouraged that I
would ever walk again, I spent a great deal of time on
the Web looking for stories of people in my situation
who had regained the ability to walk. I tried to figure
out exactly how possible that would be for me. I
quickly found out how rare it was for someone to
recover as my Dad had done. The odds were not on my
side. I found that only 0.9 percent of people with spinal

129

cord injuries make a full recovery.

I went on to a couple of spinal cord injury forums and asked members what my chances were of walking again. I posted all the little things I could do, such as wiggle my toes and move my leg in and out. Unfortunately, I never found one person who had made that miracle recovery. Most people who responded to me explained that there still is life after a spinal cord injury. Some people were using a walker to get around the house, but no one was doing anything as active as water skiing again. Searching for these stories consumed my life, and it was all I wanted to do. In the end, it only brought me down.

My brother tried to make me stop looking. Even when we were in the van, I constantly searched the Web on my smart phone. He wanted me to talk to him and stop focusing on the unknown. Every spinal cord injury is different, he said, so I couldn't compare myself to these people. He wanted his brother back.

I was turning into a zombie. Each day was the same. My dreams had been crushed, and everything I had worked for was now over. I was five classes away from graduating when I wrecked my car, but I saw no way to return to Ohio State. I didn't want to finish at the University of Akron. I had worked so hard at Ohio State, and I wanted to graduate a Buckeye.

I lost my iPod with all the music I'd listened to in the hospital. I went to the Apple Store, bought a new iPod Nano, and went home to load it up with music. Since the hard drive on my computer had crashed, I had to download all new songs.

The music I downloaded resembled my mood and was very depressing. I started to listen to it that night and broke down in tears. I remember listening to the song "Good Life" by One Republic. I used to listen to the song while I was in the shower at my old apartment, and I would sing it out loud. I was living the good life then, but now I felt like that life was taken away from me. I became more and more depressed.

A FALLEN HERO

It was hard for me once the weather got warmer and I started to see all I was missing. I saw kids ride by on bikes, and it reminded me of the 20-mile bike rides my friends and I used to take. Waterski season had begun, and my Facebook lit up with pictures of my friends skiing. It broke my heart.

The week my sister, brother-in-law, and nieces came up from North Carolina to visit, I was an absolute mess. I was usually the one to make my nieces smile, but now they were doing everything they could to try to make me happy. Nothing worked and they grew very worried about me.

My oldest niece, Morgan, sent me a handwritten letter a few weeks later expressing her concern for me. She explained to me that she no longer saw the hero I once was to her. She said I had to keep trying and pushing myself to get better. She knew I had it in me. She had seen it when I practiced my sitting balance on the side of my bed and I shattered my record by sitting up for nearly two hours. She wanted her hero back.

This letter really affected me and made me realize the negative effect I was having on my family. All they wanted was for me to keep pushing myself and to get that infectious smile back on my face. I wrote Morgan and told her how hard this was, but that I would keep trying. It was amazing how big an impact my nieces and nephews had on me. I wanted to push myself for them, and I promised I would stop at nothing. That was easier said than done.

THERAPY BACK HOME

I went to therapy three times a week, and I dreaded every second of it. The occupational therapist hooked my left hand up to an electrical stimulation device. I hoped that this would be the answer, but soon enough I realized my hand wasn't getting any better. I finally understood that I would have to rely on my right hand for the rest of my life. Therapy felt like a waste of time. My grip strength always measured zero pounds.

The physical therapist stretched me out, and we worked on things such as sitting balance and using weights to strengthen my upper body. It seemed as if all they were trying to do was get me used to life in a wheelchair, but all I wanted to do was to work on walking again. The only time I got on my feet was when they put me in the standing frame. But even then I could stand for only a few minutes before everything began to fade out. I questioned how I would ever walk again if I couldn't even tolerate standing. I gave up.

CONTEMPLATING SUICIDE

I had never been so depressed in my life, and sometimes I thought it would be better if I just ended it. I researched all the different medications I was taking and checked to see how much I had to take to kill myself. In the mornings, I screamed at my mom it would have been better if I'd died in the crash. Knowing I was suicidal, she made sure my pills were always out of reach.

I thought of other ways to kill myself. I could cut my femoral artery and bleed out. Since I couldn't feel pain, it would be an easy way to go. I also thought of driving my wheelchair off a dock and sinking to the bottom of a lake. The only thing holding me back was the thought that if I committed suicide, I'd go to hell. But I was already living in hell and didn't think things could get much worse.

My parents grew more and more worried about me and felt I needed help. I started to see my psychiatrist every week—the same guy who helped me get through the psych ward. He knew my story better than anyone. Every week I met with him and told him how I had felt during the past week. My mom sat in on the sessions with me, so I had to be completely honest. I told him I was suicidal and all the different ways I had thought about to end my life. He adjusted my medications and added an antidepressant; he also suggested that I see a psychologist to talk about my problems.

I met with a couple different psychologists that summer and shared my history. It took the entire hour to tell my story, and afterwards I felt as if they were overwhelmed. I never made it back to the second session to either psychologist. Looking back on it, I wish I had followed up with them because they might have helped me think differently. But at the same time, I felt I couldn't take anyone's advice because no one could relate to me.

MY MOM'S 60TH BIRTHDAY

That summer we took a trip up to my cousin's

place at Bay Point on Lake Erie. My entire family, including my nieces, was there for the weekend to celebrate my mom's birthday. We got a cabin right by the water. On the first day, I rode out onto a dock and looked at the lake. I could see all of the boaters pulling tubers and skiers. I could see the smiles on their faces, and it brought me back to all the good times I once had on the water. I thought about ending it right then and there. All I had to do was push the joystick forward and it would all be over. But then I thought about my family and how much they loved me. I couldn't do that to them, so I turned around and headed back to the cabin.

My mom was walking towards me, and I could see she knew exactly what I was thinking. I started to cry and told her that I did not know how much more of this I could take. She told me I just had to enjoy the weekend and that I was surrounded by people who loved me. She did not want to lose her son, especially on her birthday.

The next day we went to my cousin's place. Everyone wanted to go to the beach, but they didn't want to leave me behind. I rode my chair up to the beach and then my brother-in-law, Todd, and my brother Mike loaded me into a wagon; Todd pulled me onto the beach and positioned me in a beach chair, where I would sit for the rest of the day. I looked out over the water where my nieces and the rest of my family were playing in the waves. All I wanted to do was stand up and be out there with them. I could also see Cedar Point across the bay, which made the whole situation even more emotional.

Throughout the day, different members of my family would try to cheer me up, but there was nothing they could say to make me feel better. We took a family picture where I forced a smile.

When we returned to my cousin's, it was time for my mom to open her presents. During that time, my Aunt Barbie from Arizona talked to me and tried to comfort me. I was told that fewer than one percent of people with spinal cord injuries make a full recovery. She told me that I would defy the odds, because I always had been the person who was part of the one percent. After all, I'd been admitted to Sphinx and had won a national waterskiing championship. She told me I was a very special person and I had to believe that I could be part of the one percent. I knew I had been lucky throughout my life, but there was nothing anyone could say to make me believe that I would walk again.

As my mom opened her presents, she unwrapped a Shutterfly book my cousin Kelly gave her. It had pictures of our entire family. We all sat around her as she looked through the book. Then she turned to a two-page spread of pictures of me taken before the accident. As I stared at the pictures, I noticed how happy I was then and how miserable I was now. I cried hysterically in front of my entire family and caused a scene. No one knew what to say or do, but my niece Morgan did give me a big hug. Eventually I stopped crying, but it seemed as if any kind of real happiness was nowhere in sight.

My sister, Trisha, gave our mom a bunch of wish lanterns—paper lanterns that had a candle at the bottom. Once lit, they floated off into the sky. That night, we went to the beach as a family to light them. While they drifted into the sky, we were to make a wish. As each lantern was lit, I wished that I would walk again. Afterwards, as we went back to my cousin's place, my mom told me that she used every wish on me. I asked her what she wished for, and she said that she wished I would be happy again. I thought perhaps that was all I should have wished for, too.

When I returned home the next morning, I continued to search the Web. I looked into different therapies for recovering from a spinal cord injury. There were stories about people who were having luck using stem cells to get them to walk again. I told my dad that I wanted to use the $20,000 I had received from fundraisers to go to Germany and have stem cells implanted. He didn't trust this procedure because it had not been approved in the United States. I continued to watch video after video about people who had gone through stem cell therapy, and I thought it was the only way.

A SIGN

During the summer, I spent every day looking for a sign that everything was going to be okay. For example, I would sit outside and wait for my mom to come outside to drive me to therapy. I would say to myself that if she walked out in 30 seconds, then I would walk again one day. I would then count down from 30, and when I hit zero I would still be waiting for her. It left me very discouraged.

One day when I was with my Mom at Kohl's, I went into the restroom, looked into the mirror, and begged God for a sign that everything would be okay. Soon after, I heard the song "Keep Your Head Up" by Andy Grammer on the radio.

At this point in my journey I had no idea what

my purpose in life was. I was completely lost, but for some reason the lyrics to that song gave me a sense of comfort. I had asked God for a sign and He had responded. For once, I was not asking if I would walk again; I asked only if everything would be okay, and He responded. Had I been asking the wrong question all along? Maybe it wasn't walking that was going to make me happy. Maybe it was something else. Something more.

SEEKING SOLUTIONS AGAIN

Day after day I continued to do my research on therapies for people with spinal cord injuries. One day I came across a program called locomotor training and watched videos of numerous success stories. During locomotor training, the patient is suspended over a treadmill in a bodyweight support harness, and two people move his or her legs in a walking motion while someone else supports the patient at the hips. It has been found that the spinal cord can be trained to remember how to walk again even without the signals from the brain.

I did a lot of research on this therapy and decided it was the direction I wanted to take. I found only seven places in the entire country that offered this therapy, and one of them was the Ohio State University (now Wexner) Medical Center. I had to get back to Columbus. I could finish up school and do therapy at the same time. I called the medical center and scheduled a time to be evaluated to see if I was a suitable candidate for the program. I finally had something to look forward to and smile about.

A few therapy sessions after finding out about

locomotor training, I was extremely excited to see that the clinic where I went had purchased a LiteGait. This apparatus is very similar to what I would be using in Columbus. A Litegait is a frame that goes over a treadmill. A bodyweight support harness allows the therapists to adjust how much weight the patient's legs actually are supporting. I explained the idea of locomotor training to my physical therapist and asked him if we could try it with the new machine. He was up for the idea and set me up in the harness. I then tried to take my first steps.

The contraption was on wheels so one person pushed it across the room while I tried to take steps. The therapist set it up so I was bearing very little weight on my legs. I couldn't get any movement out of my left leg, but I was almost in tears when I saw that I was able to take small steps with my right leg. On my first attempt, I took 15 steps with my right leg.

For the next session, we put the Litegait over a treadmill, and my therapist moved my left leg forward while I took steps with my right. I took 40 steps during the second session. Then I took 104 steps. On my final session, I was up to 295 steps.

It was the first time I'd seen progress since moving my toes. Once again I believed that maybe I would one day walk on my own. I knew I was a long way from my goal, but at least I was moving toward it. All I needed now was for my left leg to start firing. I prayed that I would be accepted into the program at Ohio State. Columbus was where I belonged, and if I was going to walk again, the people there were going to help me do it.

WRITING

It would be several months before my evaluation in Columbus. Until then I had to find something to consume my time because I was tired of the same everyday routine. Before my accident, I had been writing a book about my experiences in the psych ward. I had more than 150 pages written, and I always had dreamed of publishing a book. Now my story was much more powerful, and I wanted to share it with the world.

Because I had the use of only my right hand, I couldn't type fast enough to keep up with my thoughts. It was then that I heard about Dragon, a program that uses voice dictation to help people write. All I had to do was talk, and Dragon would write for me. I spent $250 on the software for my computer and eagerly waited for it to come in the mail.

Once all the additional software I needed was set up, I got right to work. I wrote something to post on Facebook that night titled "The Crash." I explained what happened the night of the accident and what it was like to wake up and find out I was paralyzed. I did not put in all the details of the story because I wanted to leave them for my book. However, what I wrote still proved to be very powerful. Comments poured in on Facebook. Friends I had not talked to in years were telling me how I had completely changed their perspective on life and made them realize how much they had to be thankful for. This encouragement fueled me to keep on writing. I began to figure out the reason God had kept me alive. It was to reach out to people and make them understand that they shouldn't take anything in life for granted.

I wrote every day because my life finally had purpose. I spent all my spare time on my computer writing about my experiences. Writing was a great outlet for all my frustrations. I loved writing for an audience, and once I posted something on Facebook, I waited for the comments to come pouring in. I realized I was in a unique situation where I could help others and inspire them to do more with their lives. I got so much joy out of writing I couldn't stop. It was amazing to think about what I'd been through in the last year. I no longer spent my time searching the Web for success stories. I had finally discovered there really *was* life after a spinal cord injury.

By the following month, I had 150 new pages to add to the 150 pages I had written before my accident. I read through all I'd written before the accident and knew right away I'd have to scrap most of it. My mindset had changed. I was a new person.

In the years leading up to my accident, I smoked weed every day, but I still accomplished a great deal. The title I had in mind for my book was *The Marijuana Poster Child*. I believed people could still function at an optimal level even if they were high. But now, looking back on everything that happened to me, I realized that marijuana ruined me. It was what led me to my first psychotic break and treatment in the psych ward. Then it led me to my second psychotic break and to take the long drive that changed my life forever. I read that excessive marijuana use could lead to psychosis, and that is exactly what happened to me. I still believe there are medicinal purposes for the drug, but those with mental health issues should avoid it entirely. Instead of being an advocate for weed, I was now going to speak out about how harmful this drug could be.

I reflected on my college career and realized that most of what I accomplished I did in my freshman year before I started smoking weed regularly. I wondered how much more I could have done if I had never started smoking. I thought about the friendships that changed when I was constantly getting trashed. My relationship with Kyle kind of fell apart because all I cared about was getting high, and he didn't want to be around me then. The only people I was hanging out with were those who smoked weed. Although most of these people were good friends, I lost touch with friends who didn't smoke. I had to learn the hard way how bad smoking was for my mental health.

In the new book, I wanted to teach from example: what I did right and what I did wrong. I had great success in high school and college, but I also did a lot of silly things. I wanted to share every detail from my past and not hold anything back. I didn't care what people would think of me. My close friends knew I smoked all day every day, but most people never would have guessed. I'd go to work and class high, but nobody ever knew. I could function perfectly well.

It almost felt more normal for me to be high than to be sober. I drove high all the time and even studied high. I felt I could ski better when I was high. It cleared my mind, and I felt as if it slowed everything down. Weed helped me fall asleep at night and relax during the day. It was my way of dealing with stress and escaping from reality. The literature says marijuana is not physically addicting, but mentally I had to have it to get through the day

Now that I was sober, I was thinking more

clearly than I ever had. My writing had much more meaning than it did before my accident. I was a completely different person with a new head on my shoulders.

-16-
LEAVING HOME AGAIN

MAKING ARRANGEMENTS

My appointment at Ohio State was rescheduled twice, but finally the day came. I met with the doctor who evaluated me for the program. At the end of our meeting, he said that I would be a perfect candidate and asked when I wanted to start. I intended to enter school again in January—a month away—so I told him that would be a good time. I was excited, as I actually saw this program as a chance for me to get up and walk again. On top of that, I would be able to finish what I started at Ohio State. Things were looking up.

I was still pretty nervous about moving back to Columbus because there were so many logistics to figure out. I had to find handicap-accessible housing and locate people who could take care of me. I called the housing department at Ohio State to see if there was anything available for a student with disabilities. It turned out there were two dorms with rooms available that had everything I needed. They had roll-in showers and everything was handicap accessible. I asked them to hold one of the rooms for me.

My mom was still uneasy about the idea. I would need help in the middle of the night, and she didn't like that I would be alone. Providentially, around that time, I found out about a place called Creative

Living. Creative Living provided handicap-accessible housing for people with severe physical disabilities. The facility had a resident assistant program, which meant someone was available 24 hours a day to help residents with whatever they needed. All a resident had to do was press a call button and a staff member would come. This arrangement meant I would have help in the middle of the night if I needed it.

My mom called Creative Living, and they had an opening at the time. That in itself was a very rare thing—almost a miracle. We made an appointment to check it out.

We still needed to figure out what we were going to do about my nursing and aide services. For example, I'd need a nurse to come in every other day to do my bowel program. At home, I was approved for nine hours of help a day from an aide. I just needed to find the right one. We decided to go through an agency and be assigned a nurse and an aide. I didn't like the fact that I wouldn't have a choice and worried that I would end up with someone who wasn't compatible with me.

I continued to write on Facebook, and one of my friends from the waterski team followed what I posted. He shared my notes with his girlfriend, Brooke. One day, I received a random message from Brooke, who explained how much my writing had affected her boyfriend. She said he no longer complained about the little things in life after reading about all that I was going through. She knew I was planning to move to Columbus and asked me if I needed some help. She said she was an independent provider through Medicaid waiver, and she was interested in working with me. She lived in Columbus and had recently graduated from Ohio State.

Brooke came to my house one morning and watched my aide, Toy, go through the morning routine. We then went out to eat at Olive Garden to discuss the job further. On the way there, I told her the entire story about how I thought I was Jesus and ended up in a chair. At lunch I got to know her a little better and knew right away she'd be perfect for me. I told her the hours for the job, and she said she was willing to work every shift. Little did I know that this girl would become my best friend and the best thing to happen to me that year. Now all I needed was to go to the agency for a nurse.

I took the trip to Columbus with my parents to check out Creative Living. The location was perfect—right on the South Campus on Ohio State's property. We met with the director, Marilyn, and two others from the staff. They were extremely friendly and happy to meet me. They explained that Creative Living was a nonprofit organization that provided housing to people with low income and severe physical disabilities. The rent was subsidized by the government and was based on residents' income. My cost would only be a fraction of dorm fees. Most of the people living there had spinal cord injuries, so these were people I could relate to. If I were to live in the dorm, I felt as if I would be so different from everybody else. Creative Living would provide a sense of community and the support of people who had been injured for years.

My family went to see the apartment that was available. It was a one-bedroom with a decent-sized living room, a kitchen with raised countertops that my wheelchair could get under, a bathroom with a roll-in shower, and a bedroom. It was perfect for me. Since this was government-subsidized housing, the paperwork was overwhelming; we did it at home to send back later.

We still had some more logistics to figure out while we were at Ohio State. I had an appointment with the Office of Disability Services, where I was assigned to a counselor. When I explained to him what my needs were, he said transportation would be provided by Handivan. The van would take me anywhere within three miles of campus and would be my transportation to class and therapy—a huge relief because originally I thought I would have to drive my chair clear across campus in the freezing cold to get to class.

I gave the office my class schedule and the staff arranged rides for the entire quarter. My counselor also asked if I needed help taking notes. I said I would because my right hand was not yet back to 100 percent. For every class I had a note taker Disability Services paid for. This way, I could actually pay attention in class instead of focusing on taking notes. The office also arranged to have a table that would accommodate my chair right in the front of every class. Finally, I learned I could take all of my tests and quizzes at the office, and I would get time and a half. This was a major benefit because most engineering exams are a race against the clock anyway, and now I actually would have time to check over my work. I also had the support of the Office of Disability Services if my professors were not working to accommodate me. I felt much better about returning to school after meeting with my counselor. Still, I knew I was facing a difficult adjustment.

A DIFFERENT ATTITUDE

Everything was in place. I had somewhere to live, someone to take care of me, and accommodations for class. I couldn't believe I actually had the opportunity to return to Columbus and finish what I'd started at Ohio State. It gave me something to smile about; I finally felt that God was on my side. This was a huge turning point in my life. Maybe there really *was* life in a chair. At the same time, though, I was also optimistic about the possibility of walking again once I began therapy in a couple of weeks. Everything I had written on Facebook up to that point had been a reflection on the past and talked about how badly I wanted to go back in time. Now I wrote about my future and how things were looking up.

I spent Christmas with my family and went to a New Year's Eve party at a friend's. My friends and family could tell there was something different about my demeanor. I was smiling and laughing and engaging in conversations instead of wallowing in self-pity. Many, many people told me they were so happy that I was finally being myself again. All my friends and family had ever wanted was for me to smile and laugh. They were so excited that I was returning to Columbus and were curious to see if I could defy the odds through therapy.

MOVING ON TO A NEW LIFE

Moving was easy. Being in a wheelchair meant I didn't have to do anything but order people around. My parents stayed with me the first night, but they left the next morning. Mom hugged me, and with tears in her eyes, she told me she loved me. My dad also gave me a hug and told me he loved me. This whole experience brought my Dad and me much closer together. We used to never say I love you to each other, but now it was a common occurrence.

Brooke came over when my parents left, and we spent the entire day together. We got to know each other very fast and became close as we spent every day together. She was so positive, and her smile was infectious. I loved waking up to see her every morning; her positive attitude lit up the room. No longer would I complain in the morning. Brooke made me smile and laugh, and the morning routine became less dreadful now that she was around. God had sent me an angel to help me get through my situation. I became more and more enthusiastic with each passing day. I no longer felt trapped at home because Brooke would drive me anywhere I pleased. We ate out on a regular basis. We went to the mall and found things I could still do in a chair. I had a new best friend who really cared about me and would do anything for me. I slept easy at night because I knew she'd be there when I woke up.

Through a home healthcare agency, we also hired a nurse who would come in every other morning. Her name was Dionne and I couldn't have asked for anyone better. She had a wonderful sense of humor, and we hit it off right away. She, too, could make me smile and laugh first thing in the morning. I no longer dreaded my bowel program because it meant that I got to spend time with her. We developed a tight relationship, and now she just refers to me as her "Boo."

ROUTINES

Although I had (and have) the best help in the world, daily activities still can be struggles. To get ready to leave the house, which used to eat up thirty minutes, can now take nearly two hours.

I take my medications for low blood pressure and a couple of other things. After that, I can't just leap out of bed, because my blood pressure can plummet in spite of medication. My bed is raised to 45 degrees for about 10 minutes, and then I elevate it to 90 degrees for a few minutes more. I take off the condom catheter and then use the straight catheter. Next, I lie flat on my bed and have the aide sit on my legs to loosen them up.

If this is a day I do my bowel routine, which is an every-other-day occurrence, I sit on the side of the bed to make sure I'm not going to black out. I then lie back down and roll over on my side. The nurse gives me an enema; when that's done, I quickly transfer into my shower chair. She pushes the shower chair over a toilet and I sit there for about 20 to 30 minutes.

I was wiping one day when the chair fell over; I hit my head on the tile wall as I fell to the ground. My nurse hurried to call the resident assistant and together they lifted me back into my chair. It was so scary to lie helpless on the floor. Plus, lying on a hard surface feels as if everything is just pushing straight up against the bone. Since that accident, I have had my nurse come in and hold the chair while I wipe. People with spinal cord injuries have little privacy because we need help with so many things. Before my accident I was a very private person, but at this point, modesty takes a back seat.

Next, my nurse rolls me over to the shower,

where I can do most things on my own. My aide comes in to take over and helps me wash my back and legs. I always listen to music when I take a shower because it comforts me and prepares me to take on the day. After my aide helps me dry off, she takes me back to my bedroom, where I pick out my clothes. I transfer to my bed and lie there as she gets me dressed. Finally, it is time to get out of bed and transfer into my wheelchair. It's at this point that I finally feel some sort of independence. I go into the bathroom to put in my contacts. I can get my left one in on my own, but I need help with the right one because my left hand has very little function. My aide makes me breakfast, and then I brush my teeth and do my hair. It's finally time to begin the day.

The nightly routine is tough, too. I brush my teeth, take my contacts out and take my pills. I calculated that in the last year I have taken more than 3,300 pills—for spasms, incontinence, and low blood pressure. I also take multiple medications for bipolar disorder, including a mood stabilizer and a pill for depression. On the night before my bowel routine, I take laxatives and stool softeners. In addition, I take an antibiotic to prevent urinary tract infections. Vitamins, too. I put more than 10 pills into a shot glass and take them down with one gulp.

I go to the bathroom by using the straight catheter that empties into a bag. My aide then puts a slide board under me so I can transfer from my chair into my bed. I let my head fall to the pillow and the aide pulls the wheelchair away. She then lifts my legs up onto the bed and gives me my favorite blanket to cover up my top half since that is the only part of my body that I can feel hot and cold. Since my legs are so stiff from being bent and immobile all day, I have her sit on them again to release the stiffness. I've found that this helps relieve muscle spasms at night.

Next, it's time to get positioned for bed. I like to sleep on my right side, so I have my aide put a wedge behind my back to prop me up. I have a special pillow called the Side Sleeper Pro. The pillow is shaped like a candy cane and it has a hole for my ear. I got the pillow because of that hole. Since I stay in the same spot all night and don't move, there is no relief from the pressure on my ear. After a while it starts to hurt, and sometimes it's really painful. The pillow also comes around my back, which helps me sleep on my side. Next my aide puts a pillow between my legs because without it I would get pressure sores. She then puts booties on my feet for the same reasons. She positions my legs so my feet aren't top of each other.

Then comes the part that took a while to become comfortable with. My aide puts on the condom catheter; we even tape that on to ensure that it does not come off during the night. She plugs in my cell phone next to my bed and puts the fan remote and a huge mug of water within arm's reach. She also leaves a couple of Valium there in case I have spasms that keep me awake. I need the water because my spinal cord doesn't regulate my body temperature correctly; I always wake up dehydrated and usually sweating as well. She then connects the call button to my bed so that I can reach the resident assistant over the intercom system if I need anything during the night. Finally, my toes always cramp up very badly so I have her stretch them out. After that, it's time to say good night and go to sleep.

ON A BAD NIGHT

I usually fall asleep rather quickly because of my bipolar medications and the Valium unless I have spasms. My legs start to twitch and kick and I can't go to sleep. Usually, if I take a couple more Valium, the spasms will go away after about a half-hour. During that time, I stare at the wall or sometimes I pray. Most of the time, I thank God for keeping me alive and keeping my family and friends safe. I thank Him for giving me a purpose and ask for His continued help to find meaning in my life and to allow me help me reach as many people as I can.

I've had nights when I've wakened drenched in sweat because my fan has turned off. I grab the remote and put the fan on high. When I wake, I also see if my condom catheter is still on. I do not have the sensation to feel wetness from the chest down. It is always my worst nightmare to touch the sheets and find my bed soaked. When that happens, I have to call for the resident assistant.

On one particular night, the resident assistant was a different guy. I told him my bed was soaked and that I needed him to put Chux pads underneath me. I also needed another condom catheter put on. He said he wasn't supposed to help out with catheters, so I told him everything would be fine until I woke up at 7:30 A.M. He put the Chux on the bed and helped change my hospital gown. I then had him grab a straight catheter so that I could go to the bathroom before going back to sleep. I usually have the RA wipe me off, but for some reason I didn't feel comfortable asking him to do this.

I tried to fall back to sleep, but I couldn't because I felt so disgusted at being covered with urine.

Around 5:30 A.M., I needed to go to the bathroom, so I hurried to get a catheter. I elevated my bed and quickly put on a glove and tried to use the catheter. I couldn't see anything, so before I could get the catheter in, I started to pee and once again I was soaked. I didn't bother to call the resident assistant.

I woke up when my leg started to spasm at 7 A.M. My foot tapped rapidly, and my legs stiffened up and straightened out. This caused the pillow to come out from between my legs so I had to call the RA again to reposition my legs. My aide arrived at 7:55 A.M. She helped me clean up and get ready to go to the dentist. The dentist appointment lasted more than four hours because I was with a student for his board review. Never once did I get impatient during this process. My journey has taught me everything about patience.

CLASSES BEGIN

When classes started, I was a little nervous about what people would think of me. Would they be apprehensive about approaching the guy in the chair? Would girls still be attracted to me? How would people treat me? I rolled into class and made my way to the front, where a table was set up for me. My back was to the rest of the class, and I'm sure everyone was wondering what happened to me.

Before my accident, I would sit at the back of the class and make friends with everyone around me. Now it was hard to socialize since I couldn't squeeze through the desks and get around the class to talk to people. I had a hard time making new friends. All of my other friends had graduated the year before, and now I was alone. The only time I would meet new people was during a group project, but I never made a good friend. I figured it didn't matter because I was not in school to make friends. I was there to finish what I started, and I told myself that I would focus solely on school until I finished those five classes and received my diploma.

When I was in school the first time, I skipped classes all the time. It was easy to do when I blended in with everyone else. But now I stuck out like a sore thumb, and everyone would notice if I wasn't in class; skipping was not an option. I became a better student than I had been throughout my entire college career. I developed relationships with my professors that I had never experienced before. All of my professors were accommodating, and they made it as easy as possible for me to get through their classes. Several people approached me and asked me what happened to me. I was glad to share my story, and people were blown away when they were done hearing it. Being in a wheelchair actually made me more approachable; another perk is that people remembered me. I've always liked to stand out, and now I was standing out in a different way, but I liked the attention. People were friendly; they would smile, help me open doors, and clear a path for me as I went down the hall.

LOCOMOTOR TRAINING

Therapy began on the first day of classes. The therapists were excited to have me in the program. One of them asked me what my goals were, and of course I said I wanted to walk again. He then asked me to dream bigger, and I told him that I wanted to get back to waterskiing. "There you go!" he said. This brought a

154

smile to my face. I was wearing my huge national championship ring around my neck. I explained to them that I had won a national championship a few months before my injury. It was what I missed more than anything. The ring served as a reminder as what I was fighting for. I wore it every day as a conversation starter and to remind myself that I needed to work hard to achieve my goals.

There were a few actual physical therapists on staff; the rest were students in physical therapy school and some undergrads. They were friendly, and I got along with all of them. For the first half-hour of therapy, they stretched me out to get ready for the treadmill. My legs were always very stiff, and there were only a few people who were strong enough to handle stretching me. My legs generally stayed loose for a few hours after therapy, but by the end of the night I'd be back to where I started.

After stretching, they put a modified parachute harness on me, and transferred me to a wheel chair, and pushed me up to the treadmill. They hooked me up to a cable that controlled how much weight my legs would be supporting. It took three people to get me to a standing position. Two people locked out my legs, another supported my hips, and a fourth person controlled a computer that adjusted the amount of body weight support and the speed of the treadmill. It was finally time to start walking. One person stood behind me supporting my hips while the other two moved my legs in a walking motion.

In front of the treadmill was a mirror. It was amazing to see myself standing up and even more wonderful to see myself walking. I had almost forgotten what it felt like to walk. I prayed that one day I could get rid of the harness and walk on my own, but for now this was the next best thing. When people walk, their arms usually move back and forth in opposition to the leg swing. This was now something I had to think about, and it took practice to get my arm swing down. I had to focus on keeping my head up and my shoulders back.

I was to do therapy five days a week for two hours each day. The therapists made it enjoyable, and I no longer dreaded the experience. I spent 55 minutes on the treadmill every day. For 20 minutes I had to be walking. My legs had so much tone that the trainers had to switch out every minute. It was hard work for them—so much so that even in the middle of winter they had to have a fan and the air-conditioning on full blast. Once I got off the treadmill, it was time for over-ground training. Mostly, I worked on sitting balance and other things, such as mini sit-ups and trunk extensions, on the mat.

On my first day they stood me up, but it took two trainers to lock out my legs, while another supported my hips. Another was in front of me so I to rest my arms for balance. I could stand for only a few minutes before the blackout began. I was surprised I could last the entire 55 minutes on the treadmill without passing out, but that was because the harness helped my circulation. When that first day ended, I was excited to see what the future held for me.

A NEW MINDSET

Between therapy and school, I was very busy. Now that I had something to occupy my mind, I no longer focused on the unknown. I had done everything I could to walk again, and soon I would earn my degree. I promised myself I would not get down on myself if therapy didn't get me walking again. Life was too short to worry all the time. Brooke kept me happy and motivated. Being reunited with my friends made me realize that what made me happiest was being with others. I found out quickly who my true friends were. My friend Ben made it a point to hang out with me every week. Ben and his girlfriend, Erica, were always there for me. Even though we could not do the activities we used to, we still had a good time together.

Ben told me one day that he was going to propose to Erica. On the night of his proposal, he had another friend make a heart out of rose petals in front of Mirror Lake. He took Erica out to dinner, walked her to Mirror Lake, and got down on one knee. She said yes, and the first place they went after the proposal was to my apartment. That really meant a lot to me. Ben asked me if I wanted to be in their wedding, and I was very grateful to say I would.

APPRECIATING WHAT I HAVE

Classes were going great, and I was getting used to being the kid in the wheelchair. I loved it at Creative Living, and seeing others with spinal cord injuries made me really appreciative of what I still had. I am considered a quadriplegic, but I regained function in my right hand. A lot of the other guys at Creative Living were quadriplegics without the use of either hand. I was so thankful my right hand worked. I would be so much worse off without it. I was already dependent on others, but a least I could feed myself. God spared my dominant hand, and I was grateful every day.

I promised myself I would not let my injury hold me back. I realized that the most important part of dealing with a spinal cord injury is acceptance. I had to accept my situation and know that life would go on regardless of whether I ever walked again.

I continued to write my Facebook posts and reach out to my friends and family. The first Facebook entry I wrote in Columbus was titled "Finally a Smile on My Face." My attitude had finally changed from negative to positive. People were so glad I was finally happy to be alive. So many people told me how inspirational my story was to them. I helped them understand how much we take for granted in our lives and that we should take advantage of everything this world has to offer. I loved that I was changing the lives of others as I discovered God's plan for me. The reason I was still alive was to share my story and make others learn just how much they have to be thankful for.

People I had not talked to in a very long time sometimes messaged me on Facebook and told about something very difficult they had to go through; they said my strength had helped them. It felt great to be able to help others simply by telling my story. I began to think that maybe all the suffering I had experienced was worth it. Maybe it could lift others out of anxiety and depression.

I wrote on Facebook that I wanted to get involved with public speaking. Soon enough, I was contacted by my old boss at the Student Wellness Center at Ohio State. She had a speaking opportunity for me.

THE BLOG AND PUBLIC SPEAKING

Everything was coming together. I had a plan for my future. Therapy was going very well, but the dream of walking was not coming true. Nonetheless, I knew life would go on. Even if I was in a wheelchair, I still could accomplish great things. It occurred to me that I might be more successful now that I was paralyzed than I was before my accident. I had a powerful message to spread.

The biggest thing therapy did for me was make my core stronger. When I was in the hospital, I could not sit up in a manual chair. Now I was ready to make a transition. Because I didn't have any grip strength in my left hand, it was nearly impossible for me to push a manual chair. I found something called a power assist chair that has motors and wheels that make it easy to push. Insurance usually covers only one chair every five years, but the company approved a power assist wheelchair for me at a cost of $32,000 in the same year that they paid for the $48,000 power chair. I felt so much less disabled in this chair and it gave me a real workout. I no longer looked like a giant green transformer.

I was asked to introduce myself and speak at the board meeting for Creative Living. People were blown away by what I'd been through. I mentioned that I was writing a book, which caught the attention of a man named Jon. He contacted me the next day and said my story needed to be heard and he wanted to help me with that. I developed a great relationship with Jon, who helped me raise money to find an editor and publisher for the book. He also helped me start a blog to get my story out to a wider audience, which is how www.AdamHelbling.com came to be.

I had a lot to post from what I already had shared on Facebook. But the blog proved to be a much better way to get my story out. I gained a large following, which motivated me to keep writing. My writings now were very positive, and I spoke to people about perseverance and what it takes to get through a life-changing experience. I tried to motivate people to do more with their lives and to take advantage of the gifts God had given them.

Having a blog led to more speaking opportunities. My first speaking engagement was to a class at Ohio State; I spoke about my accident and how my spinal cord injury affected me. My second talk was sponsored by the Student Wellness Center. This time I told my *entire* story. When I spoke about the adjustments my spinal cord injury requires, I got out a catheter and explained what I had to do with it. I could see a guy in the front row getting a little uneasy. He eventually got up and walked to the back of the room. Suddenly we all heard a giant thud. Apparently, the idea of a catheter made him pass out. I thought my speech was over, but eventually we regrouped and I finished it. The attendees were asked to complete evaluations, and every evaluation was extremely positive—except for the poor guy who passed out. I had made a difference in these people's lives and that made me feel great. As I became more and more comfortable speaking, I couldn't get enough of it. This was my new waterskiing. I loved seeing the looks on people's faces as I told my story. People with a spinal cord injury or bipolar disorder rarely speak out about their conditions, and I wanted to be the voice of these two groups.

SPRINGTIME

Spring was upon us, and students were coming out of hibernation. From my desk I could look out my window and see students playing sports on the court about 50 yards away. They played hockey, soccer, football, and sports such as cricket, which I could watch all day and still never understand.

I wished so badly that I could get up and join in. It was hard for me to watch at times, but I think constantly seeing people being physically active was good for me. I was starting to let go and accept the fact that I would forever be left out of games like that. I spent most of my time outside socializing with the other residents, sitting in the sun, and just watching the people go by.

I sometimes found myself staring at people's feet as they walked, and I wondered why the rest of the world could walk and I was left sitting in a chair. Why would God take that ability from somebody who longboarded and skied with a body that worked perfectly? Why hadn't it happened to someone who just sat on their ass every day anyway? It seemed so unfair to me. But then I realized that I was chosen because I could handle this situation. I could take a negative experience and turn it into a positive. I could motivate others to use their bodies. God had a plan for me, and every day it became clearer.

Although it took a while to get used to seeing people riding by on skateboards or bikes and to stop wishing I could trade places with them, eventually I became content to watch. I still had my mind, and that was much more powerful than my physical self. I enjoyed the everyday conversations I had with people, and I also enjoyed meeting new people. Over time, I viewed people walking by as just more people I could help. It was good being around other people in wheelchairs because it kept me from feeling so alone. They knew exactly what I was going through, and if they could be happy, why couldn't I too?

Some things did bother me, though. When Brooke and I were on the street, people would look right past her and say to me, "You have a nice day!" The special attention was pleasant, but I didn't like being treated differently from everyone else. I think people assumed that because I was in a chair I was miserable, and their greeting would make me feel better.

I especially didn't like it when people would come up and pray for me. "Isn't it great knowing that God is going to get you up out of that chair one day?" they sometimes said. I replied that God had great plans for me *in* a chair. I explained to them about the book and my public speaking, and how God was using my story to help others. I'd tell them that I flipped my car five times and that the miracle already had occurred. God had kept me alive on that freezing cold night.

ALMOST THERE

I was very satisfied with my first-quarter grades: two A's and a B. All that stood between me and graduation were two classes. I had originally planned to pursue an entrepreneurship minor, but decided I could be an entrepreneur without classes on how to do it. The only classes I had to focus on were a fluid mechanics class and a capstone class, which included a final project.

The capstone class was split into two quarters, and during the second quarter we were assigned to work on the same project we had been pursuing the first quarter. I was extremely relieved to find out that there wasn't enough work for my group to continue the same project. The professor allowed us to choose our own project. I came up with the idea of evaluating campus to make sure that it was handicap accessible and that everything was ADA-compliant. I got our group on board, and though it took some time to convince the professor, he finally gave us the go-ahead.

We put together a checklist using the ADA compliance handbook so that we could start our inspections. We split up all the buildings on campus among five people. We found that Ohio State was amazingly compliant. The only problems we could find were that many of the buildings did not have handicap-accessible drinking fountains, and some of the bathrooms did not have sinks a wheelchair could get under. The rest were just minor inconveniences, such as having to go around a building to find the ramp. Occasionally elevators were difficult to locate. Classrooms were not set up for people in wheelchairs, but that was where the Office of Disability Services helped out. Ohio State obviously had put in a lot of thought and work to make sure the university was up to code. I did note that I always had to go to class early to make sure there were people in the hallways to open doors for me. It would've been nice to have handicap buttons everywhere, but that was not required by the ADA.

Doing this project showed me I had a unique perspective. Being in a wheelchair made me notice things no one else in the group was aware of. It also forced me to give some thought to my future after graduation. The country needed more places like Creative Living for people with physical disabilities. Creative Living was a one-of-a-kind facility, and there was a high demand for people in my situation who wanted to live independently. I decided that I wanted to get into grant writing and spreading awareness about how many more such facilities were needed. Every college campus could use a place like Creative Living.

Traveling is very difficult for people with spinal cord injuries. I thought about building vacation spots for people with disabilities that provided the same services Creative Living did for its residents. People with spinal cord injuries need a great many things when they travel. My vacation rentals would provide shower chairs and roll-in showers. I would offer vans with lifts so people could get around. I could also provide information on places that were handicap accessible to make it easier for people to plan a vacation.

I now had a new dream and a new way to use my civil engineering degree to affect the world in a positive way. I originally chose civil engineering so I could build waterski lakes, but now I would help a lot more people by building handicap-accessible housing. I'm very excited about my new dream and can't wait until one day I make that dream a reality.

Soon it was time for my final exam and presentation. The presentation for my capstone class came first, and it went very well. The professor praised us for choosing our own topic and doing it so well. At the end of our presentation, the class was to ask questions. Other groups would get only a couple of questions, but the students had a ton of questions for us. It started a great conversation, because people really hadn't thought about how much went into making the campus ADA-compliant. Our group received an A on our final project, and all that was left between me and graduating was an exam. Since I had done so well throughout the quarter, I needed only a 47 on the exam to pass the class. The exam was open notes and open book, and I had time-and-a-half to work on it. I left the exam knowing I had done it. I had graduated from college. It had taken seven years, but it was finally over. I got my grade back later that week: an A-. I would forever be a Buckeye.

GRADUATION

On June 10, 2012, my family came down for the commencement ceremony. I was part of the largest graduating class in the history of Ohio State, with more than 10,000 students receiving their diplomas. This made for a very long ceremony on a sweltering 90-degree day. The ceremony took place at Ohio Stadium, and I was the first to receive my diploma out of all of the engineering students. I then exited the stadium and went to find my family. We took some pictures and headed back to my apartment to get ready to go out to dinner. Brooke was there to congratulate me when I got home. She was very proud of me, and I couldn't thank her enough for all the help she had given me during my final two quarters. I couldn't have done it without her, and it was one of the proudest moments of my life.

-17-
CHASING THE FUTURE

It was time to pursue my dreams. The plan was already in place, and I was ready to get to work. I still was doing therapy five days a week for two hours a day, but didn't regain any movement in my legs. I was finally ready to accept that I would never walk again. I thought I would dread this day, but I found that acceptance was the key to happiness. I could finally move on and accept that the only walking I would do was every night in my dreams. A friend of mine with a spinal cord injury told me that it was foolish to dream all day about walking again. It was the same as being able to walk but dreaming all day about being able to fly.

Life became so much better now that I had accepted being in a chair. I started living. I stopped complaining and was all smiles from then on out.

I didn't work on my book much during the summer because I was writing so much on my blog. As I continued to write my posts, my words became increasingly positive. Thousands of people from all over the world were reading the blog, and many of them were telling me that it was changing their lives. My life had far more meaning that it ever had before my accident.

166

GREENLEAF

That summer I met with the Bureau of Vocational Rehabilitation, which is a government agency that helps put people back to work. They referred me to an agency called Greenleaf, which assisted me in my job exploration. I was hesitant about the experience because I thought they would see that I had a civil engineering degree and would search only for civil engineering jobs.

The experience turned out to be the opposite. I explained my dreams about writing a book, public speaking, and grant writing. They loved my career goals and told me they were going to help me meet with public speakers, grant writers, and authors.

Linda, my Greenleaf contact, set up meetings for me to meet with some very prominent speakers from the Columbus area. I had seen one of them speak a few years before; I was very excited to meet with him because I remembered that his speech had made a great impact on me. Linda and I devised a long list of questions for the interview.

I met with a lady from a speakers' bureau and questioned her, too. The one question I had for her was how much I should charge for a speech. I was astonished when she told me that with my story I should start charging $1,500 per speech plus travel expenses. When I met with the man I had seen speak before, he agreed that $1,500 was a good fee to start with. He told me he charged $8,000 per 90-minute speech. I couldn't believe there was this type of money in public speaking. I wasn't in it for the money, though. I was in it to spread my message and help people.

I decided that for now I was going to continue to

speak for free so I could get some practice. I also was on Medicaid, and if I made more than $2,000 per month I would lose benefits, which would mean I'd have to pay for my assistants and my nurses. I thought it best not to start charging until after I published my book and could support myself.

The final professional speaker I talked with was also an author. He wrote *The Complete Idiot's Guide to Success as a Professional Speaker* and had published several other books. He answered all of the remaining questions I had about speaking, and he also gave me a copy of his book, which was like the bible of public speaking. Any more questions that I had could be answered there. He also gave me insights into the publishing process.

I met with a woman who had extensive experience in grant writing. She explained that a grant writer does not need additional schooling, but had to be able to present a persuasive and justifiable case for which people would want to give money. After speaking with her, I felt confident that grant writing would be a great career option for me.

These professionals all believed in me and in my message. I returned to working on my book because so many people told me they were waiting for it.

I met with a woman from the Bureau of Vocational Rehabilitation and was approved to continue working with Greenleaf. The bureau considered me for self-employment, and with Greenleaf's help, I was to develop a business plan for public speaking, publishing my book, and grant writing.

26

It was holiday time. I was on my way home for

my birthday on December 17, but before I left, my friend Jeremy called and said he had just picked up a new husky puppy. Since I used to have a husky, I loved them, and I had to see the puppy. When we stopped at his house, I asked Jeremy to bring the dog out to the car because I didn't want to go to the hassle of getting the ramps out to get up his front steps. He told me the dog was sleeping and he couldn't bring it outside. I had no choice but to go into the house with my parents, Aaron, and his girlfriend.

I could hear a lot of noise coming from the living room, but Jeremy said our friend Jess was listening to the radio. I went into the kitchen and all of my friends yelled, "Surprise!" My brother's girlfriend had planned a surprise party for us for our 26th birthday. I'd never had a surprise party in my life, and it was a great feeling. I had a marvelous time that night, and it really showed me how much my friends cared about me. I talked with a lot of my friends that night about my plans for the future and they told me how proud they were of me.

I spent Christmas with my family and the following day returned to Columbus to resume therapy. Most people go to therapy for about four months, but I had now been in the program for almost a year. I was evaluated every 20 sessions, and each time I had made enough progress to keep going with the therapy. There were still no signs that I would walk again, but my core kept getting stronger. Even after a year, I still enjoyed participating in therapy.

A NEW YEAR, A NEW ADAM

I spent New Year's Eve with my friend Ben at a

concert. The great thing about being in a wheelchair is that you get placed right up next to the stage for concerts. After New Year's, I updated my Facebook status. Here is what I wrote:

> "Still can't walk. Still can't get myself into bed at night. Still can't run. Still can't jump. Still can't ski. I've only slept through the night once in the last two years. But all that matters is I'm happy. This has all been as much a mental battle as it has been physically, and mentally I'm winning. It gets easier every day. I don't dwell every day on the things I can't do. I love my life and what I have to look forward to. I'll publish a book this year and share this incredible journey. I'll speak out about spinal cord injuries and bipolar disorder. This is the year where I prove to God why I was worth saving. This is the year where I truly will make the difference in the world that I've always wanted to make. I ask you all in 2013 to stop and think about what you have and take those gifts and use them. Here's to 2013!"

This was the most popular post I ever made on Facebook, with 300 likes. To make good on my promise, I wrote every single day for hours on end. I drank Five-Hour Energy every day to keep myself awake to write. I was a machine, and I wrote a majority of my book in that one month.

BACK TO THE SCENE OF THE CRASH

A couple of days before the two-year anniversary of my accident, I traveled with my parents to Rushville, Indiana, to see where I crashed my car. I saw the "Jesus is Real" sign that had fueled my manic episode. I remembered that my tire blew out on I 70 W after I crossed into Indiana and that I had gone to find a gas station. I have no idea how I ended up in Rushville because it was nearly 20 miles off the highway. I surely would have passed a gas station before that.

We definitely took a different route than I did to get to Rushville. When we arrived in the city, we spent most of the time searching for the gas station where I tried to change my tire. I wanted to retrace the route on which I was speeding before the accident. We went to every gas station in the city, but we couldn't find it anywhere. We finally gave up, but along the way we saw the hospital where the paramedics had brought me immediately following the crash.

THE THINGS THAT WENT RIGHT

My dad had brought a blown-up newspaper picture of my car from the accident scene and a copy of the article that accompanied the photo. In the background of the picture were an old farmhouse and a barn. We set off to look for them. The newspaper article described the intersection where I crashed. About a mile down the road from the hospital, we found the abandoned farmhouse. There was about a five- to eight-foot hill off the side of the road where my car must have flipped.

From visiting the site, I realized there were so many ways I could've ended up dead and many so-called coincidences that kept me alive. I originally thought I was driving down a two-lane highway, but in fact it was a two-way street, and I was passing cars on the left-hand side heading into oncoming traffic. I could easily have hit somebody head on and killed them or myself if I hadn't crashed when I did. About 100 yards from the crash site were some trees next to the old barn. Had I crashed a little later, I could have ended up in those trees and most likely would have died.

When I had turned onto the street where the accident occurred, I chose to make a right turn, which took me past a police station. Two officers were walking into the station at the time; they saw me fly by and jumped into their patrol cars. Had I come by a bit later, the officers might already have been in the station and not seen me. If they hadn't chased me, the paramedics probably wouldn't have reached me in time. If I had gone left instead of right, I would've gone into town instead of into the fields and probably crashed into a business, a house, or a telephone pole, and most likely I would not have survived. Since the hospital was only a mile down the road, the medics were able to get me there and stabilize me right away. Then I was flown by helicopter to Methodist Hospital in Indianapolis, which was also nearby. It happened to have Indiana's largest trauma center.

Visiting Rushville made me see how lucky I was to be alive. I thought it would be emotional, but it only assured me that God kept me on Earth for a reason. He definitely was looking over me that night, just as I thought.

REFLECTING ON LIFE SINCE IT CHANGED

January 22, 2013, marked the two-year anniversary of my accident. I had heard that after two years, recovery from a spinal cord injury comes to a halt. I had thought I would dread this day, but I was ready for it. As I looked back on the previous two years, I was so proud of myself because I had come so far. I went from being absolutely miserable and crying to my mom every day to getting a college degree and having a smile on my face almost all the time.

I looked at a picture of myself from the ICU, which reminded me of how well I had done. I still vividly remember that first day of physical therapy when I sat up for 15 seconds and blacked out. I felt like a rag doll, and on my anniversary date, I was so much more stable. I also looked at pictures of myself lying in bed, having lost 45 pounds. I didn't even look like myself.

Today, though, I smile when I look in the mirror every morning. I see the same person I was before the accident. I tell myself to keep that smile on my face during the entire day. I now see my accident as a blessing rather than a nightmare. I feel more joy in helping people overcome adversity than in teaching people how to waterski. I accomplished enough in that sport. It was time to move on. It's great that the last time I skied was when we won our national championship. I could not have ended on a better note.

I have learned more in the past 24 *months* than in the previous 24 *years* of my life. Someone once told me that God would never give you something that is too big to handle. I realize that I'm stronger than I thought. I think most people would've given up by now and thought their lives were over. Not me. Every day I get a little closer to my dream. I have found myself through my injury, and it has helped me plan my life. Some people say that everything happens for a reason, but some people never discover the reason. I am so fortunate that I figured that out in just over a year. I was given a second chance at life, and I am not going to let that go to waste. I look at every day as a gift.

LOOKING DOWN FROM HEAVEN

One night, I was looking up at the stars and wondering what it would be like if I were looking down from heaven rather than looking up from Earth. I realized that my work here was far from over. I had won some prestigious awards and accomplished a lot in the sport of waterskiing, but what would people remember me for?

I definitely did *not* want them to remember me as the kid who smoked pot every day. I'm happy now that I can be remembered as a survivor, a fighter, and as someone who was able to turn tragedy into triumph.

I want people to realize that nothing is impossible regardless of the situation. We are all unique, and we all have something to bring to the table; we just need to find our niche. When I applied for the Sphinx senior class honorary and had to write my epitaph, I wrote, "Here lies a man that truly found happiness. He tried what he thought he'd like and pursued only what he knew he loved."

For me, that one thing was waterskiing, but once

that was taken away from me I had to search for something else. Now I find joy in helping others. There's so much for us to discover. We have to go search for it!

There are people in the world who can make us truly happy, so we don't have to be afraid to meet new people and make new friends. We have to stay away from the ones who bring us down and don't believe in us. I'm happy to say I have found a great many true friends along my journey. Although I can't be included in everything anymore, my friends take me into their lives as much as they can. When my friend Jeremy bought a house, he built a deck on the back—with a ramp—just so I could get inside. When Brooke bought a house, she made sure I would be able to get inside and move around. She wouldn't settle for anything else.

BLESSED

My family has never been prouder of me. I call my mom every day and I call my dad most days. We always say we love each other. Our family always has been extremely close. Now we are even closer. I make sure I stay in touch with them because we can never know what the future holds for us—or when.

I have been so fortunate. I can't imagine going through all that I have without the support of my friends and family. Without them, I definitely would have given up on life by now. God spared my right hand, which is a huge blessing. I am able to live independently despite my situation. I also have two of the greatest women I've ever met—Brooke and her sister, Kate—taking care of me. They are both as beautiful on the inside as they are on the outside. If I got my left hand back, I would not qualify for help, and I would not have the assistance of Brooke and Kate. That's a blessing in its way, too.

I can ride my wheelchair to therapy, which some people drive hours for. It is the best therapy I could receive in the entire country. Although I made progress on my last evaluation, it's time for me to move on after more than 600 hours of physical therapy. I'm not depressed that I didn't reach the ultimate goal of walking or getting back on my waterski. I just feel blessed I had the opportunity to be part of such a great program.

FOR MY READERS

There's a lot I want you to take away from my story. First, never feel that you are not worth anything, because God has a unique plan for you. You have to get out there and search for it because it won't just fall into your lap.

I hope it's obvious that you should stay away from drugs, including marijuana, because they can ruin your life. If you are able-bodied, be grateful and use your body. Find what you love and do it. Maybe take up waterskiing or climbing a mountain or something else that makes you feel alive. Never take the little things for granted; for example, the feeling of a hot shower. Or even the feeling of needing to urinate and then letting it all go.

The advice I always hated, but which turned out to be great advice, is not to look at what you *can't* do, but what you *can*. I've seen people such as football player Eric LeGrand living with paralysis from the neck down and still having a fulfilling life.

I challenge you to be happy. I challenge you to try something new. I challenge you to meet a new friend. No matter how hard times get, keep fighting. Help somebody today. Someone is always worse off than you, so never feel bad for yourself. However, depression and anxiety are real, so if you need help, get it. If you need medications, take them. I still take antidepressants, and if I were without my bipolar medications, I would still think I'm Jesus.

God took away my legs and a whole lot more, but His intention was not to take away my happiness. Although it would have been great to be Jesus, I don't think I would have been very good at it. And besides, it's a lot of work to be Jesus.

Someday, maybe Jesus will come back and heal me. Or maybe he'll be pissed at me because I thought I was He—twice. It has been a long struggle, but I have found peace after the storm.

I have always loved this quote by Steve Jobs, and I think it describes me fairly well:

> "Here's to the crazy ones. The misfits. The rebels. The troublemakers. The round pegs in the square holes. The ones who see things differently. They're not fond of rules. And they have no respect for the status quo. You can quote them, disagree with them, glorify or vilify them. About the only thing you can't do is ignore them. Because they change things. They push the

human race forward. And while some may see them as the crazy ones, we see genius. Because the people who are crazy enough to think they can change the world, are the ones who do."

I'm one of the crazy ones.

ABOUT THE AUTHOR

Adam Helbling was born in Akron, Ohio and was raised in Stow, Ohio. He was born on December 17, 1986 with his twin brother Aaron. His family includes his dad Bob, mom Patsy, brothers Mike and Aaron, and sisters Bobbie and Trisha. He has two nieces Morgan and McKenna, and two nephews Zachary and Keller.

In 2005 he moved to Columbus to attend The Ohio State University on a full-ride scholarship. His greatest physical passion was waterskiing and he was a national champion show skier, a state champion slalom skier, and he helped lead the Ohio State Waterski Team to win the 2010 Division Two National Championship.

He was very involved at Ohio State and in 2008 he was chosen to be a member of the SPHINX Senior Class Honorary. This honor is given to only 24 seniors at The Ohio State University who best represent the university.

He has bipolar disorder, which has led to two manic episodes. The second lead to a car accident that left him as a C6/C7 quadriplegic. The first year was a struggle, but eventually he let go of his physical passions and focused on his mind.

He graduated from The Ohio State University in 2012 with a degree in Civil Engineering. His dream now is to build more places like where he resides, called Creative

Living, for people with physical disabilities. He also wants to partner with vacation resorts to build places ran similar to Creative Living so that people with disabilities can vacation independently.

He now enjoys his time writing on his blog. He loves his career as a Motivational Speaker and a Life Coach. He believes that everything happens for a reason and is happier now than ever before.

He can be contacted at a.c.helbling@gmail.com or on his website at www.AdamHelbling.com.